THE CHRISTIAN CONSCIENCE

THE CHRISTIAN CONSCIENCE

John Y. Clagett

REGULAR BAPTIST PRESS
1300 North Meacham Road
Post Office Box 95500
Schaumburg, Illinois 60195

Library of Congress Cataloging in Publication Date

Clagett, John Y., 1935–
The Christian Conscience.

Bibliography: p.
1. Conscience. 2. Conscience—Religious aspects—
Christianity. I. Title.
BJ1278.C66C56 1984 241'.1 84-9824
ISBN 0-87227-097-1

THE CHRISTIAN CONSCIENCE

Regular Baptist Press, Schaumburg, Illinois
Printed in U.S.A.

Contents

Introduction

As Christians living in today's world we face a multitude of conflicting voices, all telling us what to do or what to believe. We are confronted with workshops, films, seminars, and self-help books of all kinds. Most of these, prepared by competent and well-meaning believers, share certain principles designed to help us achieve victories if we apply them correctly.

The field of Christian ethics is well supplied with titles dealing with the opportunities and responsibilities of the sincere child of God. Many of these offerings are how-to-do-it books and programs or testimonials that serve as models for behavior. However, there is precious little to be found dealing with the issues of motivation and the making of value judgments.

As an individual, I do not want to be told what my choice should be in a given situation in order that I may copy some leader who has books and tapes for sale! I want to know what things I need to know in order to make my own valid and successful decisions. I am an individual of average intelligence who just happens to believe that I can think for myself! I want to know what the Bible says about my options. I want to relate properly to God, and, at the same time, I want to live according to the gifts and opportunities that are mine, and for which I must give account some day.

It is impossible for me to regard God as One Who desires that all persons be exactly alike. There are no divine molds. God did not make me just like my brothers. We do not look alike or think alike. We enjoy different things, and we have varying opinions. Why should I be expected to walk in lock step with some other believer? What right have I to expect you to do what I do, or to think as I do, or to make the same choices? The Bible says that every one of us shall give account of himself, not someone else, to God. Individual responsibility is clearly taught in Scripture, and I am willing to recognize my own responsibility to serve the Lord acceptably with reverence and Godly fear.

While this strong assertion of individualism and personal discipleship sounds admirable, it may be easier to say than to do. Society has witnessed a decline in the concepts of objective authority and personal responsibility, and this decline has had a great influence on the Christian community. It is easy to assert individualism in the wrong way; we may then overlook or disregard the commands of the Lord and become guilty of denying His Lordship over us. In short, we assert ourselves without proper knowledge or skill, and then we are forced to try to defend our choices and actions. We are frustrated because, on one hand, we don't want to imitate or emulate others, but on the other, we aren't free to do everything our own way!

Appeal to Conscience

When we are confronted with the sameness and the anonymity many would have us adopt, we rebel and we do our own thing like the ancient Israelites did. Judges 17:6 says, ". . . every man did that which was right in his own eyes." The problem is that we make mistakes, as all people do, and then we try to reconcile the matter by appealing to some authority other than the Bible. We allow the Bible to remain silent or to gather dust on the piano while we appeal to something much more personal and up-to-date—our own experience. We live in a day when many people are claiming unusual and personal spiritual phenomena as part of their religious experience. The modern rise of individual claims to subjective revelation and to unique extra-Biblical activity reflects an "anything goes" mentality, which lacks Biblical support. The trend to find answers in individual experience has led many to leave careful study of the Scriptures and to turn to some other source for their sense of well-being and direction.

The individual conscience is appealed to more and more as a frame of reference for right and wrong, and we are all influenced by the trend whether we like it or not. We see our friends involved in activities that we find to be unacceptable as Christian behaviors, and they tell us that their conscience said it was all right. We find ourselves looking for some internal and informal witness to which we can appeal when we desire more freedom of choice in our own lives. Individuals are appealing increasingly to how they *feel* about a proposed activity when they either do not like what the Bible and the church have said, or they simply do not know. Perhaps you have done the very same thing.

There is a strong sense of the "up close and personal" in all of us. We like to have good feelings about ourselves and we like it when others admire us. We are personal creatures and we have personal desires and feelings. We are constantly thinking and discovering new situations and evaluating them. It is clearly true that God does not clone us all after some approved model, or make robots of us; therefore we must decide for ourselves about things. Can your conscience be trusted to guide you when you must determine right from wrong, or good from bad; can it help you to determine if the Lord is leading you?

Many people cry that the church cannot meet the needs of the people. They claim that the church is not able to relate to the individual and his needs and the issues of his real-life struggle to succeed. This is partly true. The church cannot make the choices and feel the feelings for you! You must be responsible as an individual for the way you conduct your own affairs. For example, the service station may provide quality gasoline and oil, may make maintenance checks and repairs, even provide road maps; but that is where the service stops! The driver must read traffic conditions and adjust accordingly. He cannot hold the service station responsible for his own carelessness! The church will not "drive your car" for you. When you start on a trip, do you consult a map or do you rely on your conscience to tell you which road to take?

Many Voices

Multitudes of believers attempt to use conscience as a road map to direct them through the maze of circumstances confronting them. There are some clinical psychologists who advocate conscience as a valid decision-making ally. There are many who say conscience can not be trusted. Others claim that if the conscience is properly taught, or Christianized by means of learned Christian standards, it will effectively direct the individual where the Bible is not specific.

In the depths of our inmost beings we must feel that we can approve our choices and behaviors. We must gain sufficient satisfaction somehow, and if the Word of God does not mention the matter before us, what are we to do? We all consider it to be a very personal and private matter and we jealously guard our right to decide for ourselves. Consequently we seldom ask for help or direction from those persons who may be well qualified to give it. This leaves us with what we *think* about a situation, or how we *feel* about it.

A Ray of Hope

The apostle Paul, in his letters to the Corinthian church, has given the world a precedent for relating to moral issues. The matter of conscience surfaced there as they were faced with many issues not unlike those we face today. We can examine the concept of conscience held by the Corinthians to see if it is the same as ours. We can also take a close look at Paul's ideas and statements about conscience to try to discover what the best view of conscience should be. First of all, we must accept the doctrine of the supernatural inspiration of the Scriptures and the co-Authorship of God. The result will be an authoritative statement on the matter at hand. We can then move on to discover the factors contributing to the use of conscience at Corinth and see if they are valid for us today. In short, we may be able once and for all to discover what conscience really is and how it operates. If we can do this we will have the Bible as our teacher and we will not need to resort to unreliable and often conflicting human opinion.

Certainly, one of the major tenets of Christian teaching is that of forgiveness, but what about the cleansing of a guilty and defiled conscience? How are we to be free from the continual feeling of guilt? Once we discover what we need to know about conscience we can look at forgiveness and cleansing, and at such things as the restoration of the individual, and the confidence which comes from knowing that cleansing is real and complete. We will have a better grasp of our resources and of our opportunities for living an acceptable and satisfying life. Living for God is too important to leave this great stone unturned! It is imperative that we make the best possible use of whatever truths we can find to help us live as good stewards of the grace of God.

One

The Discovery of Conscience

> And the LORD God took the man, and put him into the garden of Eden to dress it and to keep it. And the LORD God commanded the man, saying, Of every tree of the garden thou mayest freely eat: But of the tree of the knowledge of good and evil, thou shalt not eat of it: for in the day that thou eatest thereof thou shalt surely die. . . . And the LORD God caused a deep sleep to fall upon Adam, and he slept: and he took one of his ribs, and closed up the flesh instead thereof; And the rib, which the LORD God had taken from man, made he a woman, and brought her unto the man. And Adam said, This is now bone of my bones, and flesh of my flesh: she shall be called Woman, because she was taken out of Man. Therefore shall a man leave his father and mother, and shall cleave unto his wife: and they shall be one flesh. And they were both naked, the man and his wife, and were not ashamed (Gen. 2:15–17, 21–25).

The scene in the Garden of Eden must have been wonderful. God had created a perfect man in His own image and had provided an environment perfectly suited to his habitation. Adam was also given a job to do; that is, he had a purpose for living. God placed him in charge of the garden, and of all creatures (Gen. 1:26). Adam was the person commissioned by God to have dominion over all the things he could see, hear, feel and touch. His was a delegated authority from God that extended to all but one item, a certain tree that was found in the midst of the garden (Gen. 3:3). This tree was off limits to the ruler of the garden. The tree of the knowledge of good and evil was a gracious provision made by a loving God to the man He had made. It was the means by which God would remind Adam that even with all of his authority and dominion, he was still a creature. Having all authority, Adam could have easily forgotten that he was still responsible to a higher Authority—God. God's prohibition reminded Adam of God's presence, and served as a standard by which Adam could measure his job performance in terms of obedience. Adam could not have meaningfully obeyed God without that tree, because it represented the only restriction. God had provided a means by which Adam could say "I have been faithful and obedient." A gracious God had created the man, put him in perfect surroundings, and even made his existence meaningful and measurable.

Adam was innocent. He had no knowledge of wrongdoing, and had perfectly obeyed God. We do not know how long this condition existed, but we assume there was some interaction between Adam and God because of the statements made by God to Adam. There is no record of any statements made by Adam to God, unless the naming of animals constituted such statements, before the fall. We have more reason to assume interaction existed than to deny it, so we add one more gracious provision—access to God.

God knew all of Adam's needs and realized that companionship could not be found for the man from the animals which surrounded him. God made a woman and brought her unto Adam, and Adam recognized the suitable partner and appears to have been quite satisfied (Gen. 2:23). They lived together with no confusion, no guilt, no fear, and no sin. There was no sin anywhere in the physical creation; to be sure there had been sin among the angelic creation, but not yet in the world which surrounded Adam and Eve.

It is apparent there was no sense of guilt, for there was no guilt. God had created the man with all of his faculties, as seen in the fact that he could think, talk, labor, love, and make value judgments based upon God's revealed will. God had provided a reminder that some objective authority outside of Adam existed in the universe, and in so doing had provided Adam with a way to know right from wrong. It was quite simple: to eat of the tree of the knowledge of good and evil was wrong and everything else had to be right. To disobey was wrong and it carried penalties and judgment. Judgment was to be imposed by God in the event of disobedience and Adam knew it. We are not sure that Adam understood what was meant by the phrase "thou shalt surely die," for there had never been a death; yet Adam no doubt thought it was something to be avoided because it was associated with the result of wrongdoing. Adam learned from God's statements. He was conditioned by the things God said and the things God did. He knew that all was well as long as he did not eat of the tree, and perhaps he told Eve not to even touch it just as a safety measure (she reflected that in her statement to the serpent, i.e., "neither shall ye touch it"). God had not told Adam to avoid touching it, merely to avoid eating of it.

Primitive Pain

Adam's whole environment was good, his relationship with Eve was apparently good, and his interaction with God is assumed to have been good. Yet in some sense there were subjects about which he had not gained experience or knowledge. He was subject to input from his environment and could learn many things, yet there were some things he could not learn unless he disobeyed God. God had deliberately prevented Adam from knowing things which were not good for him to know. God did not want Adam to experience some things, because it would not be good for Adam to experience them. There is a great principle here for all Christian parents to recognize at this point! Even God prohibits certain knowledge and experience for the welfare of those He loves. Modern permissiveness does not follow God's precedent.

Adam knew there was a God, and he knew right from wrong. He was confronted with the concept of individual responsibility, and even with all this knowledge he allowed himself to be persuaded to disobey. The serpent had made a statement containing a veiled promise; their eyes were to be opened to new knowledge. He said, "For God doth know that in the day ye eat thereof, then your eyes shall be opened, and ye shall be as gods, knowing good and evil" (Gen. 3:5). What did that mean? Surely their physical eyes were already open! It must have meant that in some way they would experience knowledge as a result of their wrong act. In some way they would be able to recognize something they had never known before—the great difference between good (which they already knew but probably did not recognize) and evil. That day they would gain knowledge and experience something indeed, because for the first time they were to feel the pain of conscience! Conscience was awakened that day for the first time, and there were some drastic results. They experienced evil and knew guilt. They felt the inward torment of negative awareness and their lives were altered by it. Genesis 3:7 says: "And the eyes of them both were opened, and they knew that they were naked; and they sewed fig leaves together, and made themselves aprons." Their relationship with each other was changed and they were not able to feel the same openness with each other. Some have suggested that they felt naked toward God—that is, exposed in their guilt—and that the fig leaves were an attempt to mend their relationship with Him. There is not sufficient evidence in the text to support such a view. They were clearly not able to relate to each other as before. Verse eight is most instructive: "And they heard the voice of the LORD God walking in the garden in the cool of the day: and Adam and his wife hid themselves from the presence of the LORD God amongst the trees of the garden." The sound of God's presence as the wind blew softly in the garden struck fear into the hearts of the first pair for the first time. Perhaps God came often to the garden in the evenings, and perhaps it was a time when Adam related to God all that had taken place; but not this time! They hid themselves. Why? Adam's answer is clear, as seen in verse ten: "I heard . . . I was afraid . . . I was naked; . . . I hid myself." God said: ". . . Who told thee that thou wast naked?" Adam had experienced the torment of conscience, and he was able to know guilt, fear, and a sense of need before God. There is no evidence that he had learned this from any other creature or from any angel; certainly not from God! Adam had learned to recognize conscience. Apparently he had within him a faculty that was able to inflict pain of some kind, and it operated automatically when he became guilty. We remember data and we remember events with what we call memory. Memory can be trained and used at will. Not exactly so with conscience. **Conscience can be conditioned, as Adam's was conditioned by God's statements about the tree, but it cannot be controlled by man's will.** We cannot turn conscience on or off, because it acts automatically. Adam was afraid for the first time because he was aware of guilt and of the consequences of guilt. His act had activated his conscience. Aparently it was there all the time, created with him, but it had not acted because Adam had never disobeyed before. He had never had the eyes of conscience opened until he had, in fact, become guilty.

A Common Problem

Adam's problem is not his alone. All of his offspring are born with the knowledge of good and evil, in the sense that they inherit Adam's nature. Adam was changed from a creature who was sinless and innocent, created in the very image of God, to a creature who was sinful and guilty. The image was marred! Adam's posterity inherits the image of a man who is a fallen being; one who is a sinner before God (Gen. 5:3). Ephesians 2:1 describes mankind as ". . . dead in trespasses and sins." Romans 5:12 traces the source of the problem back to Adam: "Wherefore, as by one man sin entered into the world, and death by sin; and so death passed upon all men, for that all have sinned." Mankind the world over has the knowledge which Adam gained that fateful day in the garden: we all know that God exists and that we are in need before Him. We are aware of guilt and of its consequences and we are afraid. So we hide ourselves from a holy God. We have inherited not only Adam's nature, but his conscience as well.

All over the world the results of this universal conscience toward God can be seen. Traversing the centuries of time there is the witness of man's efforts to appease God, to try to make peace with Him. We have the evidence in the Bible, which tells of the offerings of Cain and Abel, the Tower of Babel, the gods of Egypt, the human sacrifices of the Canaanites, the many temples of the idolaters, and the religious profusion of the Greeks and the Romans; and we have the contemporary witness of the people in the world around us. From the ancient Mayans of South America to the candles and prayer wheels of Europe and Burma, the profuse attempt of mankind to satisfy God is evident. Whether we prostrate ourselves many times per day toward Mecca or stand for hours at the wailing wall in Jerusalem, we can not absolve ourselves of our sense of need before God. Romans 2:11–16 says:

> For there is no respect of persons with God. For as many as have sinned without law shall also perish without law: and as many as have sinned in the law shall be judged by the law; (For not the hearers of the law are just before God, but the doers of the law shall be justified. For when the Gentiles, which have not the law, do by nature the things contained in the law, these, having not the law, are a law unto themselves: Which shew the work of the law written in their hearts, *their conscience also bearing witness,* and their thoughts the mean while accusing or else excusing one another;) In the day when God shall judge the secrets of men by Jesus Christ according to my gospel (italics mine).

Thus, it can be seen that man is trying throughout his years and throughout his universe to capture in some small sense the peace that Adam knew before the fall. He tries all the time and uses everything at his disposal, but he still is not satisfied. Before the fall Adam built no altars, and he sacrificed no animals. He built no temples and he prayed no prayers. Why? The obvious answer is because he did not feel the need to make peace with or to placate God in any way. He had no guilty conscience at that time.

A Confused Answer

Mankind is endowed with something else beside conscience—ingenuity. The many kinds of worship devices and the multitude of totems and altars is ample testimony to his inventive mind. Man may be alienated from God, but he is not lazy toward God.

There appears to be a lack of satisfaction concerning the major intangible issues of life, and this dissatisfaction has caused people to become very inventive as well as tolerant toward non-Biblical religious practices. The lack of satisfaction may be traced to many factors on the worldwide scale and in our own society. Around the world nations struggle to feed their people and to provide security for their boundaries. They maintain concentrated vigilence toward everyone and are forced to adopt attitudes not conducive to feelings of trust and well-being. People live daily in fear and with the tangible concerns of survival. As they endure they are aware that things could be better. They ask themselves why things are so unsure, and why there is not more security, and if there is a god, have they somehow angered Him? The solution to the last of these problems is to invent or deify and idealize a concept of God and seek to worship the concept. The idea behind the practice is to appeal to some person or force outside the limitations of their own setting, who will provide some encouragement or assistance in their struggles. The search for an objective God goes beyond the search for physical help, such as rain when it is needed, protection from enemies, or answers at the time of death. It extends to the provision of something to believe, something in which to place one's confidence, something to worship. If and when the structure of beliefs is threatened in some manner, people feel the need to polarize and defend their beliefs. When our security is threatened we become hostile and we react strongly. So it has been throughout history, relative to worship. The ark of the covenant was the central piece of furniture in the ancient tabernacle of the Israelites. It was the place of meeting between God and the high priest. It was kept securely in the inmost area of the tabernacle and regarded as most holy. The ark represented God's presence among His people, and it served as a rallying point for worship, for leadership, and even for battle at times. First Samuel 4:3–8 affords insight into the issue:

> And when the people were come into the camp, the elders of Israel said, Wherefore hath the LORD smitten us to day before the Philistines? Let us fetch the ark of the covenant of the LORD out of Shiloh unto us, that, when it cometh among us, it may save us out of the hand of our enemies. So the people sent to Shiloh, that they might bring from thence the ark of the covenant of the LORD of hosts, which dwelleth between the cherubims: and the two sons of Eli, Hophni and Phinehas, were there with the ark of the covenant of God. And when the ark of the covenant of the LORD came into the camp, all Israel shouted with a great shout, so that the earth rang again.
>
> And when the Philistines heard the noise of the shout, they said, What meaneth the noise of this great shout in the camp of the Hebrews? And they understood that the ark of the LORD was come into the camp. And the Philistines were afraid, for they said, God is come into the camp. And they said, Woe unto us! for there hath not been such a thing heretofore. Woe unto us! who shall deliver us out of the hand of these mighty Gods! these are the Gods that smote the Egyptians with all the plagues in the wilderness.

It appears that even the Israelites, who had been carefully taught not to respect idols as objects of worship, were dangerously close to regarding the ark in such a manner. It was synonymous with the presence of God. There can be no question that it was regarded in such a manner by the idolatrous Philistines. The concept that God was present provided great encouragement for the Israelites and great fear for their enemies. They gained great security from the idea that God was on the scene and that God was on their side in the battle. They shouted their joy, so great was the confidence.

Men have invented representations of gods in many forms, but they all have the same purpose: to provide security and to give worshippers an object for their faith. Another case in point is the encounter by the apostle Paul and his companions at Ephesus:

> For a certain man named Demetrius, a silversmith, which made silver shrines for Diana, brought no small gain unto the craftsmen; Whom he called together with the workmen of like occupation, and said, Sirs, ye know that by this craft we have our wealth. Moreover ye see and hear, that not alone at Ephesus, but almost throughout all Asia, this Paul hath persuaded and turned away much people, saying that they be no gods, which are made with hands: So that not only this our craft is in danger to be set at nought; but also that the temple of the great goddess Diana should be despised, and her magnificence should be destroyed, whom all Asia and the world worshippeth. And when they heard these sayings, they were full of wrath, and cried out, saying, Great is Diana of the Ephesians (Acts 19:24–28).

The point here is security. They were in danger of losing their livelihood as well as their confidence in Diana. They reinforced each other by asserting the greatness of Diana. The inventiveness of man is also seen in the doctrine they held concerning Diana:

> But when they knew that he was a Jew, all with one voice about the space of two hours cried out, Great is Diana of the Ephesians. And when the townclerk had appeased the people, he said, Ye men of Ephesus, what man is there that knoweth not how that the city of the Ephesians is a worshipper of the great goddess Diana, and of the image which fell down from Jupiter? Seeing then that these things cannot be spoken against, ye ought to be quiet, and to do nothing rashly (Acts 19:34–36).

Notice the assertion of the greatness of Diana by means of mass hysteria, the appeal to common knowledge as documentation and to the idea of universal belief as proof, the idea of an image from Heaven, namely Jupiter, and the idea that the doctrine was indisputable. All these are mechanisms for the defense of the concepts of the people's religious beliefs. To lose confidence in Diana was to lose their sense of security; therefore, their exhibition and assertion of common belief served to reinforce them. Their religious God-consciousness and their sense of need before God were assuaged by substitute worship. There was superstition but not genuine satisfaction toward God. There was religion, but the guilty conscience toward God remained.

The answer to the issue of man's conscience is also confused by simple adjustments we make to issues in our own society. For instance, the American family structure has seen great change in the last seventy-five years. Years ago we gained a great deal of our security from the relations we had as large families remained together or lived in close proximity to each other. We are now a very cosmopolitan and mobile nation and we are often removed from parents and other relatives (and roots) by many miles and by the passage of long periods of time. Activity outside the home is the mainstay of teenage life, especially in urban areas. The moral breakdown and the rise of secular humanism has challenged the best thinkers as they attempt to cope with change. With change comes an attempt to explain what was, what is, and what will be. We look at our views and ask questions about them, and we hear new ideas which seem to make sense. The resulting frustration only points out the continuing sense of shortcoming and the need for security. We speculate that there may be merit in such things as the study of oriental transcendental and metaphysical religious effort in order to discover some secret to peace. We invent, as did the ancient Athenians, our own unknown gods and we wonder if perhaps we might be correct. Perhaps God is made in man's image rather than the other way around. Speculation is dangerous, and it affords no authority but that of its possessor, no substantiation but the feelings of its adherents, and no proof other than the insistent declarations of those who have no options—they must believe or lose their panacea. The sense of need still remains after the dust of a thousand golden calves has long settled, and the silence blankets the soul like the fearful shroud of death. We cannot satisfy our own need for peace with God by means of invention or ingenuity, because we know within ourselves the futility of self-effort, our conscience bearing witness with quiet insistence.

Social theories have been posed as an alternative to the problem also, in that they are tied to learned experiences. We are told that what we have learned as right and wrong may be right and wrong for us, but not for other persons without the same training. In short, the majority view is regarded as normal, so any deviation from the majority view is abnormal. Abnormal is viewed as unproductive and hurtful, and therefore wrong for the individual. According to this view there are no absolute rights or wrongs; instead all is relative to the way things are regarded by the majority of people in a given population. According to this view, when the majority of the Germans thought it was right to exterminate the Jews, then it was right to do so. It can be easily seen that to trust in the majority opinion as our source for standards leads only to more confusion and error. Conscience is more than the sum total of our learned experiences; it is a way God has chosen to impart to all of us truths about ourselves, about His existence, and about our relationship to Him and to others. It is not derived from social theory and cannot be removed or silenced by social considerations.

The scene, then, is a confusing one; however, God is not the author of confusion. God would have us know what is meant by the references to conscience made in the Bible and He would have us be equipped to explain the issue to others. We must ask the correct questions and study carefully to discover the correct answers. We must also be willing to allow ourselves to be taught. We must accept Scriptural statements as authoritative, even when they run contrary to what we have been taught or to our cherished opinions. We must be willing to discover the true nature of conscience and to see how it works if we are to profit from this study.

Two

The Concept of Conscience

Derivation of the Idea

The term for conscience used in the Corinthian epistles is *suneidesis.* Any attempt to trace its meaning, as with other New Testament terms, would normally lead the researcher to try to discover its use in the Old Testament. As we search the Old Testament, however, we discover that this Greek word has no direct equivalent in the Old Testament Hebrew vocabulary. The closest idea to this word for conscience is found in the use of the word "heart." There is a good example of this use in the situation describing King David's experience as he felt the inward pain of an accusing conscience. His heart "smote" him. Now, we are not to suppose that David was having a heart attack—he was having an attack of conscience! Second Samuel 24:10 says David's heart, or conscience, was smiting or bothering him as a result of what he had done. He felt the great discomfort of knowing his guilt. He had done wrong, he was guilty, and he was feeling anxiety as a result of it.

Even though the word for conscience does not appear in the Old Testament, the concept of conscience is clearly there. Job 27:6 says ". . . my heart shall not reproach me . . . ," using the same idea of the heart as the seat of inward torment. The Babylonians also identified conscience with the heart, as did the Egyptians who had no word for conscience but, as is evident from the Book of the Dead, did recognize its authority. The early Greeks and Romans personified the concept of conscience, and depicted it as fiendish female demons. To the Greeks conscience was Erinyes, and to the Romans, the Furies.

If the idea of an accusing conscience was well known, it was just a matter of time until the proper label would come forth to identify it. That occasion came at about 200 B.C. when Greek-speaking Jews who lived in Alexandria, Egypt, were given the task of translating the Old Testament, with its ancient Hebrew language, into a more modern Greek version. Their work, called the Septuagint (meaning "seventy" because seventy men worked on the project), has the very first use of the word *suneidesis* in Biblical literature to refer to conscience. How did it develop? When translating Ecclesiastes 10:20, the translators attempted to fit a Greek concept to the Hebrew word *maday,* meaning thought or knowledge. It means a bad thought or negative knowledge in the context. The verse says: "Curse not the king, no not in thy thought; and curse not the rich in thy bedchamber: for a bird of the air shall carry the voice, and that which hath wings shall tell the matter." Ecclesiastes was written in the tenth century B.C., but it was translated into the Greek by Philo in about 150 B.C. The word *thought* carried the idea of conscience, as we know it, and associated wrongdoing with negative inward feelings and with the idea that someone else would find out about the wrongdoing.

Aquila viewed conscience, or negative mind, as the *scene* of cursing, but the pagan Greeks regarded it as the *agent* of cursing. This slight difference allowed the idea to surface that conscience is not merely the *place* for negative thought, but the actual *means* for the thought. Conscience came to be regarded as a part of man, a faculty like memory, and not merely the content of negative memory.

The Nature of Conscience

The word *suneidesis* comes from the root verb *sunoida,* which in turn comes from the root *id.* It is the root for the verbs *to see* and *to know,* and the prefix *sun* means "with." Literally, then, the word for conscience means "to see with," or "to know with," and the scope of the knowing is with oneself. What the word meant in the Corinthian epistles is to know with yourself, and it is usually understood to mean the same thing today.

But what is the actual nature of conscience? Modern concepts of conscience are very broad and carry ideas that do not agree with the Biblical view at all. It is important at this point to establish the clear understanding that the nature of conscience as reflected in the Bible identifies it as a faculty or part of man. It is not merely the sum total of what a person learns, or a societal norm, or a cultural standard that has been learned.

Webster defines conscience as a "knowledge, or sense of right and wrong, with a compulsion to do right." Related to the word *conscious,* the idea is that the individual knows and is mentally aware. This modern concept sees the conscience as a mere accumulation of knowledge but not as an inborn part of the individual. Have you ever heard someone say "Let your conscience be your guide"? Modern views of conscience presuppose that the conscience is some kind of ever-present friend and advisor who warns of poor choices and encourages good choices. Conscience is often pictured in television commericals as a transparent facsimile whispering to a housewife so that she will use the prescribed product instead of brand X. On other occasions conscience is an angel advising the good, or a horned devil saying, "You really did it this time!" or, "Go ahead, it won't hurt you."

Secular humanism, which pervades the thinking of so many people today, would have us believe that there are no moral or ethical absolutes, and therefore no objective right or wrong behaviors. The current view absolves man of guilt by reducing his moral responsibility to near zero. Corporate responsibility rather than personal responsibility has become the standard. The will of the majority is right and the narrow views of the religious conservative are regarded as sources of irritation and therefore wrong. In liberal religion the views of the many are regarded as correct due to sheer numbers, without regard for "Thus saith the Lord."

The depersonalization of God by society has served to remove the sense of responsibility and the consciousness of sin. When God is remote the concepts of sin and accountability are reduced to a mere matter of unproductive choice. The general and vague ideas of conscience common today are quite compatible with unregenerate society, and if the correct and Biblical view of conscience is to be recognized there will be the risk of ridicule and rejection. It is imperative that the intelligent and concerned Christian discover what the Bible says about the faculty known as conscience. Its nature and function must be carefully studied. Does God use the human conscience? If so, how? Under what circumstances? Can the Christian rely on his conscience as a guide? Can it guide if it is sufficiently Christianized?

The New Testament Evidence

The use of the word *suneidesis* in the New Testament seems to be directly related to the Hellenic world, specifically Corinth. Since the word is used most often by the apostle Paul, with reference to the situation of believers at Corinth, it is not unreasonable to regard the use of conscience as an important factor in Paul's ministry there. That conscience was a unique and important issue at Corinth is indicated by the application of the term to that city more than any other place mentioned in the Scriptures.

The word *suneidesis,* or conscience, is used thirty times in the New

Testament.[1] Nineteen of these are found in the writings of Paul, five appear in Hebrews, three are found in the letters of Peter, two in Acts, and one in the Gospel of John. Paul used the word more than any other writer of Scripture. In addition to the nineteen times Paul used *suneidesis* in his undisputed writings, many scholars think he was also responsible for its appearance in the book of Hebrews. If Paul was the author of Hebrews, he would have been the user of the word *suneidesis* in twenty-four of the thirty occurrences in the Bible. It is also noted that Paul did not use the word in his writings prior to his letters to the Corinthians. He later used it in his epistle to the Romans, but only after the concept had been clearly exposed; and he wrote from Corinth dealing with issues similar to those dealt with in that city (cf. Rom. 2:14, 15). We conclude that the concept of conscience was surfaced, refined, dealt with, and introduced into the Christian vocabulary by Paul as a direct result of the needs of his ministry at Corinth. If we are to understand the New Testament concept of conscience we must learn what it meant to the Corinthians, and study Paul's use of it there.

Kahler deals with the use of the term by the apostle and its introduction into Christian usage:

> It was introduced into the primitive Christian vocabulary by Paul, outside of whose letters it occurs in the New Testament only in the Acts (in Paul's mouth), in I Peter, and in Hebrews. In his work Paul comes in contact with the general human conscience (II Cor. iv. 2), and appeals to it (Rom. ii. 15; xiii. 5, 6), or corrects deviations in it proceeding from remnants of heathen ideas (I Cor. viii. 7; x. 23 sqq.).[2]

The "remnants of heathen ideas" mentioned above are referred to as "gentile presuppositions" by C. A. Pierce:

> It must be said at once that there is every indication that among these presuppositions there stands that which can be summed up in the catch-word conscience.
>
> Up till now in his ministry, so far as his surviving writings, or, for what it is worth, the author of Acts, attest, he has not used the word. It is now forced on him by the exigences of his ministry.[3]

Pierce further states that the "inference is irresistible, that conscience was introduced into Christianity under pressure from Corinth, as bound up with a controversial issue."[4]

E. A. Sophocles, in his *Greek Lexicon of the Roman and Byzantine Periods,* defines conscience as the "judge."[5] In calling conscience a judge, Sophocles identifies the concept used at Corinth during the time the Epistles were written. The Corinthians relied on conscience to judge their actions, and they lived accordingly. Paul encountered this use of conscience at Corinth and built his arguments to the Corinthian people around it. This function of conscience is attested to by Kahler also:

> It makes them morally independent by a self-judgment which penetrates to the most hidden motives (Rom. ix. 1; II Cor. i. 12), coordinate with that of the Searcher of Hearts; and it is capable also of passing judgment on others (II Cor. v. 11; iv. 2).[6]

It appears that conscience was mostly negative in its role and that it was active after an act was committed, not prior to the act. A man was not guilty until he had acted, so a negative and accusing conscience could not operate until he was, in fact, guilty. Bascom says: "The conscience is identified by its negative witness to existing sin, which is in concord with the pagan-Greek concept of conscience."[7] When referring to the writings of Ignatius, Bascom describes: "His usage of suneidesis reflects the common idea of associating sin or wrong-doing with the subsequent effects upon conscience."[8] The word *suneidesis,* or conscience, then, is used in its commonly understood role of bearing witness after the fact to wrongdoing. This idea of the conscience acting only after the guilt or the activity is supported also by Sanday and Headlam in their careful commentary on Romans. They declare that it:

> . . . is somewhat more restricted than that which obtains in modern times. Conscience with the ancients, was the faculty which passed judgment upon actions *after they were done* . . . , not so much the general source of moral obligation.[9]

Conscience is seen to function, then, as the result of misdeed, as an automatic built-in accuser over which man has no authority.

Some have argued that Paul compared the Gentile conscience of Romans 2 with the Mosaic Law of the Jews. This comparison is clear in the matter of condemnation, or lack of condemnation, but there is no warrant for the supposition that the comparison is to be carried into other areas. This is done by some in an attempt to demonstrate that the control of conscience is volitional, or subject to the human will; and that conscience operates antecedently. C. A. Pierce notes this contrast between the Biblical view of conscience and the modern view of an antecedent conscience thusly:

> But conscience in Greek, and the N. T. offers no exception to this, does not look to the future: its reference is to acts at least begun, if not irrevocably completed, in the past. It tells me that what I have done is sin.[10]

Conscience does not operate before the fact or the action of the individual; therefore, it is impossible for the conscience to lead, or to instruct, or to advise, or to tell anyone anything ahead of time! Let us settle it, then, that we are not to trust conscience to come to our aid in a decision-making activity. Paul recognized that it does not work that way, and we should recognize it also. Sometimes we confuse the function of memory with what we suppose is conscience at work. It is quite possible to remember the pain of conscience as experienced on a previous occasion, and to associate that memory with the anxiety felt, as wrongdoing is anticipated. To put it simply, we remember the awful feeling of guilt we had last time and we feel new anxiety because of what we remember. It is also true that we experience feedback anxiety as we contemplate an action which we know to be wrong or worthy of punishment. An example can be seen in the sweaty palms, the quickened heartbeat, and the backward glance of the wrongdoer just as he begins his act. These experiences are not the work of conscience, but of memory and of judgment.

Conscience, then, is seen to be negative when it functions as a result of one's misdeed. On the other hand a "good" conscience equals no sense of guilt, which, in effect, is no conscience at all. A good or clear conscience is an unaroused accuser, a sleeping dog. **Conscience comes into operation on the commission of a bad act, and when no such act has been committed, it remains dormant.** The content of *suneidesis,* then, is expected to be negative or bad on the one hand, or empty and void on the other. Hence a good conscience is not a positive one, as compared with the norm, which is bad, but is a neutral, void, or inactive one. An excellent example of a silent conscience is that referred to by Paul when he said "For I know nothing by myself; yet am I not hereby justified: but he that judgeth me is the Lord" (1 Cor. 4:4). Paul is saying that he knows of nothing for which he should feel guilty, nothing against himself. He has no sense of guilt—a clear conscience; yet he goes on to say that his clear conscience is no basis for justification in any way. He is not to interpret the absence of guilt as a positive statement that what he had done was good or right. That kind of pronouncement must come from the Lord. Paul sought to live in such a way as to avoid arousing the activity of conscience; he wanted to live in all good conscience as he attests in Acts 24:16: "And herein do I exercise myself, to have always a conscience void of offence toward God, and toward men." In Acts 23:1 Paul said: ". . . Men and brethren, I have lived in all good conscience before God until this day." **A good conscience is a conscience that is inactive, silent, and void of any negative judgment.** A good conscience is not some form of supposed approval, or some supposed intimation of the future.

The Biblical View Summarized

The Biblical view of conscience stands in clear contrast to the modern general view. Any attempt to define conscience as taught in the New Testament involves three topics: its nature, its function, and its reference. As to its nature, it has been shown to be an element of human nature found in all persons, even those who have not had the traditional Judaeo-Christian standards of right and wrong by which to fashion their behavior. Romans 2:14 and 15 describe the function of conscience in untrained and untaught Gentiles as part of God's indictment of all persons. They are said to have a conscience toward God and that each conscience functions by bearing witness. Concerning this verse Alfred M. Rehwinkel says: "Conscience is innate. According to Rom. 2:14–15 conscience is innate and universal. It is not the product of environment, training, habit, race impression, or education, though it is influenced by all of these factors . . .[11] B. H. Nadal also supports this view:

> It has no origin but that of its possessor; it is born with him, though from its nature it is only developed farther on in life, just as reason and imagination are. It has been asked, in reply to this view, whether conscience is not made what it is in any given case by the circumstances about it—by teaching, by the man's own acts—in short, by all the influences brought to bear upon him. We answer it is as to its form, but there was first conscience, a moral faculty in the man to be shaped. We concede that neither moral ideas, nor ideas of any sort are innate; but the capacity, nay, the constitutional necessity for moral ideas is innate.[12]

Apparently man has within him a faculty which responds to his actions by tormenting him when he becomes guilty of wrongdoing. To assume that conscience can act volitionally is unwarranted, and there is no evidence whatever of an independent conscience or of an intelligence other than the conscious mind of the individual. There is only one mind, one heart, and one will per individual.

The function of conscience has been shown to be that of accuser, or judge, which condemns the guilty or remains silent when no guilt is present. Conscience can only point out guilt, never well-doing. It can act only after the fact and never before, and is therefore not capable of advising as to future action.

The reference of conscience has not been dealt with at length because it will be handled in the following chapter. Suffice it to say that the reference is to the order of things in society, the possibility of conditioning being freely admitted, and the need for an accurate standard for Christian behaviors is seen as crucial to all acceptable service.

Notes:

1. W. F. Moulton, and A. S. Geden, "Syneidesis," *A Concordance to the Greek Testament* (Edinburgh: T. & T. Clark, 1897), 160.

2. M. Kahler, "Conscience," *The New Schaff-Herzog Encyclopedia of Religious Knowledge*, IV (1952), 242.

3. C. A. Pierce, *Conscience in the New Testament* (London: SCM Press LTD., 1955), 64.

4. Ibid., 66

5. E. A. Sophocles, "Suneidesis," *Greek Lexicon of the Roman and Byzantine Periods*, I, 1042.

6. Kahler, "Conscience," 242.

7. John Carroll Bascom, "*Syneidesis* In the New Testament" (unpublished Th.M. thesis, Dallas Theological Seminary, 1962), 35.

8. Ibid., 22.

9. William Sanday and A. C. Headlam, *A Critical and Exegetical Commentary on the Epistle to the Romans. The International Critical Commentary* (Edinburgh: T. & T. Clark, 1895), 61.

10. Pierce, *Conscience*, 114.

11. Alfred M. Rehwinkel, "Conscience," *Baker's Dictionary of Theology*, ed. Everett F. Harrison (Grand Rapids: Baker Book House, 1960), 136.

12. B. H. Nadal, "Ethics," *Cyclopaedia of Biblical, Theological, and Ecclesiastical Literature*, III, 321.

Three

The Conditioning of Conscience

The Possibility of Conditioning

Conscience has been said to be innate and God-given. We have seen that it functions as a judge of deeds committed, and as an executor of the punishment for the offense. We have referred to the modern views that relegate conscience to mere learned experience. To what extent are the modern views valid? Does learned experience play an important part in the subsequent development of conscience? The answer is "yes," we are very much affected by what we are taught and led to believe about right and wrong. Our environment is filled with activities and experiences to which we relate in a number of ways. Some things we avoid because we have learned that they are hurtful, such as the handling of hot items. We feel pain and we learn from the pain. Alexander Pavlov demonstrated that this procedure works even in animals, using sounds and pain to condition behaviors in dogs. David Seabury, a modern clinical psychologist, explains how the conscience is conditioned:

> We know that when we become enmeshed in an environment and have taken on its thought patterns, it is difficult for us to open our minds to attitudes in wide contrast with those to which we have become habituated. This rigidity is caused by what are technically known as coenotropes: that is, centers of prejudice and ideas toward life on which the mind has become set, to which it attributes special values and toward which it turns as inevitably as steel is drawn to a magnet.[1]

The average conscience is conditioned by family opinions, and social biases and prejudices—even the Christian conscience! The delusions and superstitions of a particular time and place affect all of us and create either tolerance or intolerance for certain persons, activities, or ideas. For example, consider the Christian young person who is reared in the deep South. This young person grows up in a cultural environment which frowns very keenly upon the practice of exposing the body in public. Consequently, the sincere Christian will not wear shorts in public, even when others who are friends feel quite free to do so. This same person, reared where the raising of tobacco is a way of life and many respected Christian people smoke cigarettes, will allow the practice and not feel that it is wrong. These same two issues, nudity and smoking, are viewed in quite a different way by the Christian who is reared in the North. This person will openly appear in public wearing shorts and will not feel guilt at all because it is commonly practiced in his environment. He will, on the other hand, as a sincere Christian, experience guilt and feel pain if he smokes a cigarette! Good Christians just do not smoke in the North, but they do in the South!

God's Conditioning

While we recognize that man may condition his own conscience by his exposure to culture and to the teachings of a given society, social interaction is not the only conditioning factor. It appears that God also conditions the conscience of man. This inward court has been called an ethical sense organ by some, and the categorical imperative by others, such as Kant. We would expect a universal conscience to witness to a common sense of need in man as he relates to God. Romans 1:20 says "For the invisible things of him from the creation of the world are clearly seen, being understood by the things that are made, even his eternal power and Godhead; so that they are without excuse." For man to understand his position before God, and to know that he is without excuse, is to confront the issue of universal spiritual need. When Romans 2:15 says "their conscience also bearing them witness," we must understand that it is a witness to existing guilt and that somehow God has so presented His claims as to condition the conscience of every person to some degree. The very existence and authority of God is demonstrated in nature according to the words of the Psalmist:

> The heavens declare the glory of God, and the firmament sheweth his handywork. Day unto day uttereth speech, and night unto night sheweth knowledge. There is no speech nor language, where their voice is not heard. Their line is gone out through all the earth, and their words to the end of the world (Ps. 19:1–4).

The apostle Paul also addressed the issue of God's witness to all persons when he said: "Nevertheless he left not himself without witness, in that he did good, and gave us rain from heaven, and fruitful seasons, filling our hearts with food and gladness" (Acts 14:17). Perhaps the most striking statement of God's universal declaration of Himself as a wrathful God is that found in Romans 1:18, 19:

> For the wrath of God is revealed from heaven against all ungodliness and unrighteousness of men, who hold the truth in unrighteousness; because that which may be known of God is manifest in them; for God hath shewed it unto them.

There are many who will deny the existence of God, but the Bible clearly says that all persons are made aware of His existence and that the message is understood. The pride of unregenerate man will lead him to construct excuses for himself, however invalid they may be, and will lead him to deny the moral-religious consciousness he feels.

God has not relied solely upon nature to accomplish the task of prior conditioning in every man's conscience. The universal work of the Holy Spirit is also said to be a contributing factor. Genesis 6:3 says: "And the LORD said, My spirit shall not always strive with man. . . ." What was the work of the Spirit prior to the flood? What striving did God perform? Perhaps it was not unlike that promised in John 16:8, where Jesus is reported to have said: "And when he is come, he will reprove the world of sin, and of righteousness, and of judgment." We may conclude, then, that this inner self-attestation of God is the result of God's activity in man, and that it is witnessed to by conscience, producing in every man what Delitzsch calls "inalienable knowledge about his moral reciprocal relation to God."[2]

Cultural Conditioning

Perhaps we fail to realize the extent to which conditioning occurs as a result of our own choices and activities. We live in a culture which dictates for us many things we must accept if we are to be successful. What young man is not influenced by the challenge of patriotism? We inherit by virtue of being born in a certain time and place the established mores that are present. We live in a free country, with clearly established democratic principles that are a part of our way of life. We make choices for ourselves that expose us to specific influences, some of which are very influential and determine our future experiences. The choices we make are not made in a vacuum, but in a society pregnant with opportunities and fraught with dangers.

As shown earlier, Paul surfaced the concept of conscience in ancient Corinth. Corinth was not really very different from the cities of modern

America. Their culture did much to condition them and to create attitudes of right and wrong. Many factors were present in their rich and cosmopolitan environment that are also present to confront us today. They were influenced by philosophy, mystery religions from the East, insecurity, the breakdown of moral values, rationalism, and scientific advance to name a few. They had a vast pantheon of religous voices, materialism, and humanism also. They were confronted with the widespread practice of adultery, as well as fornication and homosexuality. It is true, however, that they did not have automobiles and television with which to contend.

It would be well at this point to examine some of the Corinthian influences and to compare them with ours in an attempt to fully realize the conditioning factor. Among the philosophical issues of their day was Epicureanism. The chief idea of this element centered around pleasure, which was the gratification of self and absence of pain. T. Rees describes the views of the Epicureans thusly: "The aim and end of life for every man is his own happiness, and happiness is primarily defined as pleasure."[3] The situation in Greece at the time of the writing of the Corinthian Epistles was a rapidly changing one, as is ours today. They felt deep insecurities about the future and were placing emphasis on the present. While they did not have the atomic scare and the energy crisis, they had recently lost their independence to the Romans and were not looking too far into the future for their satisfactions. Rees describes their situation:

> The breaking up of the Gr city-states and the loss of Gr independence had filled men's minds with a sense of insecurity. The institutions, laws and customs of society, which had hitherto sheltered the individual, now gave way; and men demanded from philosophy a haven of rest for their homeless and weary souls. Philosophy, therefore, became a theory of conduct and an art of living.[4]

The Corinthian was trained in the art of selfishness as a consequence of this Epicurean philosphy. Life centered around the gratification of self, and social relationships were ordered to fulfill that end. We experience this today in our materialistic society. We need to own things that bring us pleasure, to do things that entertain us, and to have the constant applause of others. This desire to have something, to do something, and to be something is not new; it is even described in the Bible as ". . . the lust of the flesh, and the lust of the eyes, and the pride of life, . . ." (1 John 2:16). Note the following description of the effects of this philosphy on social life:

> Friendship, the supreme virtue of Epicureanism, is based upon the same calculating selfishness, and is to be cultivated for the happiness it begets to its owners. The fundamental defect of the system is its extreme individualism, which issues in a studied selfishness that denies any value of their own to the social virtues, and in the negation of the larger activities of life.[5]

The Epicurean philosophy, then, and our own society's self-centered, pleasure-seeking outlook on life are quite similar in their causes and effects. They both issue in an inactive social conscience and indifference.

Stoicism was also prevalent at Corinth during the first century. In nearby Athens, Paul encountered some of the Stoics at Mars' Hill (Acts 17). Perhaps the chief characteristic of the Stoic philosophy was the emphasis it placed upon reason. The Stoics pursued knowledge about ultimate problems as a rule of life, and they were always ready and willing to hear any new thing. To them the pursuit of dialogue and traffic in religious information were especially valuable. They held that the law of nature (logos) was the principle of intelligence in man, and the divine reason immanent in the world. Theirs was a form of metaphysical pantheism, which considered all the world as God, and every part of it divine and worthy of worship. The Stoics were very religious with reference to ethics. They were perhaps the most "moral" of the early pagan people of Greece; but their morality was relative, being conditioned by their relative view of evil.

The Stoics correspond in almost every detail to the great influences of the amalgamation of religion in our society. The tolerance of modern man toward sin and degradation is merely a reflection of the absence of moral absolutes. This attitude is quite compatible with the view of the Stoics that all is relative, that all of us worship the same God, that careful and Biblical doctrine is dispensible, and that dialogue is the chief end of religion. We are conditioned by Ecumenism and by an inclusivistic attitude to the extent that we allow the unregenerate to think that all is well, and that they have no spiritual need. The conscience of modern man is desensitized to a great degree by his culture.

Partially related to the Stoic thought was the element of Gnostic influence. The value of knowledge was understood by the Corinthians, and they felt that to possess a high degree of understanding was emancipating. If the Stoics had a form of Process Theology, the Gnostics had Liberation Theology! Paul deals with this issue in 1 Corinthians 8, with relation to the eating of meat in the idol's temple. Conscience is very much conditioned by knowledge, and Paul discovered the relationship of knowing a thing to be wrong and doing it anyway, to that of doing something with the confident assurance that it is all right. We are forced to realize that what we think—that is, what knowledge we have—will determine the activity of conscience. Our knowledge comes mainly from our cultural orientation.

Another influence which has a counterpart in our society was the profuse religious practice of the Corinthians. As stated, they were quick to seek knowledge for the sake of having knowledge, but they gave little serious thought to incorporating restrictions on their behavior. Their pantheon consisted of many gods and they were influenced by the mystery religions which came their way from Asia. Theirs was an amalgamation of religious teachings and practices that often contradicted itself. The basic problem could be traced to the fact that they had no unified body or systematic teaching of doctrine. Paul said they were too superstitious, and he was quite correct, for their beliefs were no more than superstitions allowing each person to construct his own ideas about the gods. He then mixed his own ideas with those inherited from others. Fisher describes the gods of the Greeks:

> The gods in Homer are human beings with greatly magnified powers. They are males and females, each class having the characteristics of the corresponding sex among men. Their dwelling is in the sky above us, and their abode on the top of Mt. Olympus. They have bodies like those of men, but their veins, in the room of blood, are filled with celestial ichor. In size they do not, generally speaking, surpass the human measure, but sometimes they are spoken of as gigantic.[6]

The Corinthians created gods in their own images. They were thought to experience hunger, to need sleep, to acquire knowledge, to be placated by a human sex act as worship, and to be capricious in their dealings with humans. It follows that if their gods were not holy, or careful in their behavior, the mere humans who followed them did not need to be holy or careful either. The point is this: they had no absolutes, no standards, no commands, no teachings, no Scriptures, no restrictions on behavior at all. They actually used sex in worship with temple prostitutes as they worshipped Aphrodite, the goddess of beauty and love. The many forms of worship are partially described by W. H. S. Jones:

> There were no sermons and few prayers in Greek worship. Its object was, not to edify the worshipper, but to persuade the god or goddess to grant a favor. The chief means employed of persuading the deity was burnt sacrifice, processions, dances and hymns.
>
> It should be noticed that there was no priestly caste. Many of the priesthoods were held by girls and women, and, with very few exceptions, no ministers of the gods laid claim to peculiar sanctity.[7]

As evidenced from the discussion above, there could have been no unity of belief or doctrine concerning moral behavior. Even gods were subject to moral deviation, and no standard involving restraint was to be found.

Personal Conditioning

We have seen that conscience is trained in many ways. As shown previously, conscience cannot act antecedently but can only act after the fact of guilt becomes actual. It is plain that God conditions the human conscience and that we inherit cultural influences that condition our consciences. But to what extent do we condition our own consciences? The pain that we experience as a result of misdeed will either be great or small, depending on our religious or cultural opinions about what we have done. If we are quite sincere about obedience to God, and we take His prohibitions against a particular act, such as adultery, to be strong and emphatic, we will experience strong guilt feelings when we violate those prohibitions. Psalm 51 is a classic example of a case of moral lapse with the strong feelings that accompany guilt:

> Have mercy upon me, O God, according to thy lovingkindness: according unto the multitude of thy tender mercies blot out my transgressions. Wash me throughly from mine iniquity, and cleanse me from my sin. For I acknowledge my transgressions: and my sin is ever before me. Against thee, thee only, have I sinned, and done this evil in thy sight: that thou mightest be justified when thou speakest, and be clear when thou judgest. Behold, I was shapen in iniquity; and in sin did my mother conceive me. Behold, thou desirest truth in the inward parts: and in the hidden part thou shalt make me to know wisdom.
>
> Purge me with hyssop, and I shall be clean: wash me, and I shall be whiter than snow. Make me to hear joy and gladness; that the bones which thou hast broken may rejoice. Hide thy face from my sins, and blot out all mine iniquities. Create in me a clean heart, O God; and renew a right spirit within me. (Ps. 51:1–10).

In the passage just cited, King David, who has been guilty of lust, adultery, and murder by proxy, is crying out to God for forgiveness and cleansing. He asks to be purged and to be given a clean heart and a right spirit. He speaks of truth in the inward parts, and he has lost all joy, knowing that God has been instrumental in the producing of these great dissatisfactions and guilt feelings. It should be noted that all of the parts just mentioned are relating to inward and non-physical sources of pain. He is suffering from the effects of a guilty conscience, but has not yet learned to use our modern word for it.

We have shown the reaction by conscience to David's sin in order to demonstrate what happens when the individual has a clear and strong sense of God's standards, and yet violates them. It appears that when the standards and prohibitions are strong and clear that the conscience reacts more strongly, producing greater pain. The statement David made attributing the "bones which thou hast broken" to the work of God focuses our attention on the possible use God makes of the guilty conscience. David's amplified guilt can only be explained by the idea that the Holy Spirit is at work, using the known standards and the faculty known as conscience, to bring David to the place of repentance and confession. Apparently He was successful!

But what happens when the individual does not have standards and beliefs that permit his conscience to react negatively? Is it possible to silence the effects of conscience by simply refusing to believe? The answer is a qualified "yes," because we all believe many things that we have learned from parents and from our culture, not to mention the prior conditioning by God. Yet, we do silence the voice of conscience to some degree by refusing to allow ourselves to be confronted by God's standards. A case in point would be the young person who does not like the restrictions of a Christian life-style, and does not like to have pressure placed upon him by the church. He can solve his difficulty by simply not attending any church. He can refuse to read the Bible and he can obtain material from some other religious group with much more liberal expectations. Or he can ignore all religious teachings and become completely secular in his interaction with society. In other words, he can change the standards! To be sure, he does not change God's standards, but he changes his own relation to them. The ultimate example of this is the self-proclaimed atheist, or in the case of society's standards of behavior, the sociopath.

As a person rejects standards he becomes an anarchist, or a rebel of sorts, and launches out in a lonely world of rebellion. He adopts a life-style that says "I don't care" and lives with attention on only the present. He usually applauds humanistic ideas that reinforce his own ability and independence, and loses his concepts of moral decency. **To attempt to silence conscience by ignoring the standards only leads to debauchery.**

The individual may condition his conscience to remain silent in yet another way. The Bible describes this method in action: "Now the Spirit speaketh expressly, that in the latter times some shall depart from the faith, giving heed to seducing spirits, and doctrines of devils; speaking lies in hypocrisy; having their conscience seared with a hot iron. . . ." The apostle Paul, who knew the concept of conscience better than anyone else in his day, told Timothy that it is possible to "sear" the conscience. Paul's use of this imagery surfaces the concept that continued and flagrant violation of standards will gradually produce insensitivity. It will become easier to sin each time the sin is repeated, because the role of conscience becomes less actively felt. Literally, Paul is speaking of what we may call "conscience burn-out." This conditioning of the conscience does not happen suddenly, but rather over a long period of time. It is the little foxes that spoil the vines of conscience. This usually happens when the less critical issues are violated, and the attitudes are more open or tolerant. We sin, and because the matter is either one about which we are not too concerned, or one that is done in secret and we do not wish to expose ourselves, we do nothing. We simply choose to endure the discomfort of conscience rather than repent, confess, and seek restoration. As we become more and more accustomed to living with a guilty conscience we grow insensitive to its urgings. We sweep the conscience under the rug and go on as if nothing is wrong, gradually forsaking the careful attitudes we once had. A modern example of the way we become desensitized can be seen in the increased use of profanity, violence and sex in public entertainment. It has become commonplace to use four-letter words and slang expressions. We have open display of illicit sex and the flaunting of moral inhibitions in every medium from the printed page to prime time television. Christian people, who claim to love Christ, God and the Bible, and who accept the Christian life-style in modern society, are increasingly casual and indifferent to the trend. The Christian conscience is less sensitive as a result of living with violations until those violations become commonly accepted ingredients of the culture.

In the passage cited above, the phrase "giving heed to seducing spirits" seems to accurately describe the problem. We hear and we allow ourselves to be enticed, with the resulting hypocrisy. We choose to live with it because it has become easier to live with the problem than to struggle against it. Individuals become habituated to the mores of their environment. If those mores are permissive and place no restrictions on behavior, the combined absence of standards and desensitized conscience will allow those individuals to feel as if nothing is amiss.

Notes:

1. David Seabury, *How Jesus Heals Our Minds Today* (Boston: Little, Brown and Company, 1949), 182, 183.
2. Franz Delitzsch, *A System of Biblical Psychology*, trans. by Robert Ernest Sallis (Edinburgh: T. & T. Clark, 1899), 160.

3. T. Rees, "Epicureans," *The International Standard Bible Encyclopaedia*, ed. James Orr, II (1929), 964.

4. Ibid.

5. Ibid., 965.

6. George P. Fisher, *The Beginnings of Christianity* (New York: Charles Scribner's Sons, 1916), 76.

7. W. H. S. Jones, trans. "Introduction," Pausanius *Descriptions of Greece*, I. Loeb Classical Library (London: 1931), xxii.

Four

The Problem with Conscience

The Fallacy of Dependence Upon Conscience

Much of the problematic behavior of the Corinthian believers recorded in the Epistles can be understood only by a study of their backgrounds. They had problems with Gnostic attitudes, divisons, carnality, judging each other, going to law with each other, fornication and incest, homosexuality, idol worship, personal indulgence, selfishness, misuse of gifts, false doctrine and money. In addition the Corinthian conscience was conditioned by the Greek concept of God (having many unstable and impious gods), and by the practical outworking of those concepts with reference to morals. Their actions were free from the censoring finger of an aroused conscience because they had no authoritative standard by which to evaluate their behavior.

We must understand how the absence of standards relates to the Corinthian use of conscience if we are to understand Paul's approach to the problem. The rule of the Romans over such a proud people as the Greeks met with resentment and an unwillingness to cooperate on the part of the people. In 146 B.C. the Roman general L. Mummius captured Corinth, razed it to the ground and enslaved the population. The male population was killed, the women and the children were sold into slavery and for the next hundred years the city lay in ruins. Corinth was rebuilt under Julius Caesar, and by the time Paul arrived in the middle of the first century the city had once again become a thriving trade and cultural center. However, the people were not allowed to forget that they belonged to the Roman Empire. They paid taxes and yielded to the legal system of the Romans. Corinth was the capital of the newly-formed province of Achaia, and Gallio was the Roman deputy, or Proconsul. On his second missionary journey, Paul was brought before this same Gallio by his Jewish accusers on his first visit to Corinth (Acts 18:12–17). From the attitude of Gallio we can see something of the attitude of the Romans with reference to law enforcement:

> Although Gallio extended his protection to the Jewish religion as one of the religions recognized by the state, he contemptuously rejected the claim of the Jews that their law was binding upon all. In the eyes of the proconsul, the only law universally applicable was that of the Rom [sic] code and social morality; . . . Even the subsequent treatment meted out to Sosthenes, the chief ruler of the synagogue, was to him a matter of indifference.[1]

The Romans were jealous of their code and of social morality, but they cared little about the petty problems and differences of the people. The people were allowed to choose their own path as long as it did not conflict with the dictates of Rome, which were political and legal in their application. Gallio's behavior seems to have been normative, for Kerr observes: "he merely displayed an attitude characteristic of the manner in which Rom governors regarded the religious disputes of the time."[2] This same attitude is evident in Lysias (Acts 23:26–30), in Felix (Acts 24:22–27), and in Festus (Acts 25:1–12).

As a result of this rather general oversight by the Romans with reference to religious disputes, there was no set standard for the people to use as a guide for their actions. Rome exercised no authority with reference to these things. They did exercise authority in the civil realm concerning disputes in legal matters. There is evidence of this in the fact that Corinthian believers were contesting with each other before the unbelievers (1 Cor. 6:1–6). The people of Corinth were forced to look to their religion for some sort of standard, or moral and ethical teaching, by which to govern their lives. But, as has already been shown, the religion of the Corinthians had very low or even nonexistent moral standards. Their religion was eclectic by nature and offered no consistent form of doctrine or teaching concerning personal behavior. Pierce notes:

> It is clear that conscience only came into its own in the Greek world after the collapse of the city-state. The close integration of politics with ethics, with the former predominant, was no longer possible: there was no sufficiently close authority, external to the individual, effectively to direct conduct.[3]

To the Corinthian people there was a freedom from restraint which allowed them to do whatever they wished as long as they did not run afoul of the Roman law. This left them to seek, as did the Epicureans, personal pleasure as the highest goal of man. They were free to roam intellectually, philosophically and religiously, yet there was a basic insecurity that caused them to desire some sort of direction external to themselves. There was none to be found. When they could not appeal to an external authority, they resorted to the testimony of conscience as the judge of their actions. That such a trend toward the use of conscience prevailed in Greece is indicated by the comments of C. A. Beckwith. He declares with reference to conscience that:

> . . . it acquired its later meaning gradually in the course of the process which led the ancient world from unthinking obedience to traditional custom up to the appeal to the inner tribunal of every man's heart.[4]

However, as already shown, their conscience had already been so conditioned as to excuse their excesses and was able only to reflect the general witness of God in the heart. Such a witness pronounced them to be guilty and further compounded the problem.

Conscience has been shown to be a judge which points out guilt. Romans 2:15 shows that such a judge was operative with reference to the Gentile position before God. This accounts for their general dissatisfaction with their relation to God and explains their profuse religious effort. The Corinthian conscience was unable to function specifically due to the lack of set moral and religious standards. The people performed improper acts and felt no conscience, no guilt. Conscience was silent when it should have condemned sin. It remained dormant and the people developed a certain sense of security from the silence. This condition of self-complacency toward moral and social issues was reflected in the church at Corinth because the people were not sufficiently separated from the influences of their background. Ramsay says: "They had by no means shaken off all the habits of thought instilled into them by pagan parents and surroundings when they became Christians."[5] The church did not view the instance recorded in 1 Corinthians 5:1–8 with unusual concern. There is no mention of a guilty conscience or even the slightest sense of wrongdoing with respect to this instance of incest. Paul even upbraided them saying that they were guilty of ". . . such fornication as is not so much as named among the Gentiles . . ." (1 Cor. 5:1). Other people do not even talk about such a thing, yet these people accepted it without question! Self-satisfaction toward moral and social decay such as this can only be traced to an inactive, vitiated conscience.

This description of the impotent Corinthian conscience is not to be confused with the "weak" conscience of 1 Corinthians 8:7, 12. The former refers to the mass of unconverted Corinthians, and the latter to the recent converts in the church. It is true, however, that the weak conscience of some in the church is only slightly removed from the former state pictured above. The difference is traceable to the event of conversion and the subsequent influence of the Christian standard that was introduced by Paul.

Salvation and Conflict

When individuals experience regeneration they become new creatures (2 Cor. 5:17), and they have new interests. They desire to please God and to follow proper paths of obedience to His will. These Corinthian people, like people today, needed to be taught concerning those things that God would approve and those things that would be wrong for them. Commentators today often make the mistake of regarding the Corinthian believers as backslidden or carnal due to regression in the things of the Lord. They had not *returned* to carnality; they had never yet become emancipated from pagan ideas and practices. They were only recent converts, none more than five years old in the Lord, when Paul wrote his first letter to them. They were still working their way through the new standards provided for them by the apostle when he founded the church.

When Paul arrived in Corinth, from Athens, he associated himself with Aquila, a Jew who had recently come from Italy "as a consequence of the edict of Claudius banishing the Jews from Rome."[6] While living and working with Aquila, Paul reasoned in the synagogue every Sabbath and persuaded the Jews and the Greeks (Acts 18:4). When the Jews opposed themselves and blasphemed, Paul said, "Your blood be upon your own heads; I am clean: from henceforth I will go unto the Gentiles" (Acts 18:6). Paul moved to the house of Justus, which was right next to the synagogue (Acts 18:7), and eventually Crispus, who was the chief ruler of the synagogue, believed on the Lord with all his house. Many of the Corinthians, hearing, believed and were baptized (Acts 18:8). These are the first recorded converts at Corinth and they believed as a result of hearing Paul's teaching. The household of Stephanas was probably among them (1 Cor. 16:15). Being reassured by God in a vision, Paul stayed and taught the Word of God for a year and a half. After some trouble with Sosthenes, who had become the new chief ruler of the synagogue (Crispus being rejected due to his new faith in Christ), Paul "tarried there yet a good while" (Acts 18:18). It is clear, then, that Paul taught and preached in Corinth for more than a year and a half, and many of the people were converted. This group formed the nucleus of the church there. The teaching of Paul became the new standard by which they were to govern their lives and by which the Corinthian conscience could begin to function.

As the new believers began to try to live by their new and careful Christian standards they encountered the pain of conscience. They began to feel guilt when they sinned because they now had knowledge that certain activities were wrong for them. They did not all acquire the same amount of knowledge at the same time, and the resultant disparity is reflected in the conflict over the eating of idol meat (1 Cor. 8:4–7). With reference to the problem of meats and the fact that conscience depended on basic knowledge Pierce attests:

> . . . conscience is to some extent regarded as dependent on an assessment on other grounds of the quality of acts. In this case it is knowledge of the source of the meat eaten that brings on the pain, not the eating of the meat. Even in its negative and limited function, conscience does not so much indicate that an act committed is wrong, as that an act 'known' (by other means, and rightly or wrongly) to be wrong, has been committed.[7]

Paul, with his teaching and preaching as an apostle of Christ, provided knowledge that served as the basis for the conscience of the Corinthian church.

Salvation made a great deal of difference in the life of a believer at Corinth because his whole code of morals was to undergo an expected transformation. It is not unreasonable to recognize that a change of ethics was just as difficult for them in their day as it is for us today. Habits and ethical evaluations are deeply rooted in any society and must have represented no little problem, the results of which are reflected in the Corinthian Epistles. Into this situation Paul injected the high ideals of the Christian faith. This new ethic, or rule of life, no doubt stirred the conscience of the people as they came to accept the standards and yet fell so far short of them in habitual practice. There were many conflicts created and it fell to conscience to mediate, or decide by accusing the wrong, and to influence the believers to avoid the forbidden things. Perhaps in no other city in man's history has so rapid an adjustment and re-evaluation of ethics and morals taken place. Little wonder that there were weak brethren and divisions at Corinth (cf. 1. Cor. 1:10—4:20; 8:7, 12)!

The Wrong Use of Conscience

Paul founded the church at Corinth in A.D. 50. The probable date of the Corinthian letters is five to seven years later, about A.D. 55 to A.D. 57. There is little information about the church at Corinth during the silent years. Paul mentions a "previous epistle" in 1 Corinthians 5:9, which is no longer extant, but the subject of the letter is revealed by

Paul's statement to be the problem of fornication. Considering the vile background of the Corinthians this does not come as a surprise. They were given to this practice at the time of his first visit. As has been shown, they even did this as a means of worship.

It was during these years that conscience became a prominent issue among the believers at Corinth. Our previous discussion has shown that conscience was unreliable before their conversion due to the conditioning it received at the hands of culture, and was an ineffective judge of behavior. We also demonstrated that Paul's teaching provided a standard by which the Corinthian conscience began to act as a judge for the believers. From this beginning the issue of conscience had become a major factor by the time of the writing of the first epistle. This is evidenced by Paul's constant reference to conscience in the letters.

During this period of about five years, questions arose in the church concerning what the people should and should not do. The interference from their culture, and the absence of available and updated teaching dealing with their current issues, prompted them to seek Paul's counsel by means of a letter to him in Ephesus. He mentioned the letter in 1 Corinthians 7:1. Divisions and controversies were evident (1 Cor. 3:3, 4, 6, 8; 10:16–33; 11:17–34; 12:12–31). The battle cry of the troublemakers was "conscience," as attested by C. A. Pierce:

> . . . in the Corinthian Church external authority was in dispute and, thence, in disrepute; and, once again, its members fell back on conscience. St. Paul, therefore, recognizes that it is useless to appeal to any pronouncement of authority.[8]

This line of reasoning is further strengthened by the fact that Paul nowhere refers to the Jerusalem decree, issued just three to four years earlier by the Council of Jerusalem, which dealt specifically with Gentile behavior (Acts 15:29).

To properly understand Paul's approach and his argument, it is necessary to discover what the people were doing at Corinth with the conscience issue. They were depending upon a silent conscience for approval of their deeds. Since the inward discomfort and pain brought to bear on the soul by the conscience is an after-the-fact experience, it remains that if the individual does not commit such an act he will not be bothered by the pain and discomfort mentioned. Understanding that *no* conscience concerning an act equals a *good* or *clear* conscience, they were also assuming that the absence of pain and guilt feelings could mean that the act was a good act and that it should be approved. In short, when no remorse was experienced after an act they assumed that the act was all right.

First Corinthians 8 provides a good example of this kind of dependence upon a silent conscience for approval. It is a case where knowledge that an idol means nothing emancipates the individual from the negative reactions of conscience. That some claimed this knowledge is clear from verses 1-6, for the apostle needed to point out that not all men had this knowledge (v. 7). Paul disapproved of their use of this freedom from conscience because their liberty, which resulted from an emancipated conscience, was becoming a problem to the weak brother (vv. 7-12). The weak brother was one who did not have sufficient knowledge of the vanity of idol worship to afford him freedom from conscience. His conscience is described as weak (v. 7) because it still reacted negatively to the practice of eating meat previously offered to idols.

The clear conscience of those with knowledge (vv. 1-6) is a strong conscience, contrasted with the weak conscience of the one who has insufficient knowledge. It follows that the strong conscience is the silent or inactive one; the weak conscience is the overly sensitive one lacking the emancipating benefits of sufficient knowledge. Robertson and Plummer support this view:

> It is just because he is feeble in insight and character that this following of a questionable example 'builds up' his conscience in a disastrous way. His conscience is not sufficiently instructed to tell him that he may eat without scruple, and yet he eats.[9]

Thus it follows that the emboldened conscience of verse 12 is nothing more than Paul's way of saying that the weak brother is led astray by the example of the one who misused his liberty. When the weak brother experiences an 'emboldened' or strengthened conscience, it is the result of improper example and not of valid knowledge gained. The weak brother assumes that he can proceed and will not be bothered by conscience, only to find that silence does not prevent him from doing wrong. After the act he is overcome with guilt because he still believes that there is some spiritual value to idols. The weaker brother's conscience does not prevent wrongdoing because it cannot act antecedently, it can only remain silent. The stronger brother's conscience does not prevent him from misusing his liberty because it remains silent also, for the same reason—it cannot act beforehand.

To depend upon the clear conscience as a sign of approval or as a green light to future activity was clearly nonproductive and invalid. The error of the Corinthians was that they used the conscience as a guide to future action, which is not its function. It does not have a volitional, but a judicial function. The use of conscience was entirely a negative one; that is, it was always either negative or silent but never positive.

Paul pointed out to the Corinthians that they were not concerned with whether their behavior was good or acceptable; instead they were using the rationale that there was no witness to their wrong deeds. This was an argument from silence, a claim that deeds were permissible if there was no condemning conscience involved. This was a negative use of a conscience that could say nothing, or could condemn an act, but could not lead in a positive way. Bascom substantiates this negative use of conscience thusly:

> From the preceding sources it appears that conscience was viewed as the fountainhead of mental anguish. Here the absence of the pain from conscience is made the basis for attesting pure motives. It suggests that the only *pure* conscience which the pagan knew about was one which was *free of guilt*. This implies that they knew nothing of a conscience which bore an actual witness of commendation. The criteria of evaluating conscience then is negatively-biased.[10]

If we understand it correctly, we are not to rely on signals from conscience to guide us because no such signals are possible. We are not to trust an enlightened conscience to help either, because it either condemns an act previously committed or remains silent. The strong brother with the liberty to partake was not advised or prevented by his conscience. The result was that he proceeded to act to the detriment of his weaker brother. We have pointed out that the conscience of the weak brother was the more active one because it lacked sufficient knowledge to permit it to remain silent. Should we desire the active conscience without knowledge so that we would be more careful of our activity? The answer is "no" because the weak conscience is an undesirable one since it troubles the brother when it is not necessary. Since the weak conscience (1 Cor. 8:7–11) is identified as overly sensitive, and since Paul instructs believers not to ask questions that can arouse the voice of conscience (1 Cor. 10:25, 27), two conclusions are forced upon us. First, it is evident that it is considered undesirable for one to have a weak conscience. The weak conscience is over-scrupulous or oversensitive. The weak conscience is undesirable because it is the result of insufficient knowledge. This is proven in 1 Corinthians 8:7, where Paul states: "there is not in every man that knowledge: . . . and their conscience being weak is defiled." Another reason the weak conscience is undesirable is that it is easily defiled. A weak brother can be misled too easily by the example of another with the result that his conscience is defiled (1 Cor. 8:7) and wounded (1 Cor. 8:12). One cannot grow positively in the Christian life if he stumbles easily over unnecessary issues or is fearful and critical of those who are able to lead him to greater victory and liberty.

The second conclusion which must be realized is this: Paul insists that **the voice of conscience is to be avoided if at all possible.** Conscience condemns a wrong act and pronounces the perpetrator of the act guilty, and it is Paul's wish that believers be spared this experience. Paul is emphatic about this, for he says: "Wherefore, if meat make my brother to offend, I will eat no flesh while the world standeth, lest I make my brother to offend" (1 Cor. 8:13). This attitude is the basis for Paul's appeal for voluntary restraint by the stronger brother, and for his admonition to "ask no questions for conscience sake," in 1 Corinthians 10:25, 27. This principle also applies to the host in 1 Corinthians 10:28 that he should not suffer at the hands of conscience (v. 29).

Since the weak conscience is undesirable and its voice is to be avoided if possible, it is clear that Paul teaches the believer to not depend upon the weak conscience to assist him in daily living. If the believer would have to commit sin before conscience could be felt, then it is not an effective deterrent to sin. Paul's appeal, as will be discovered, is directed toward the use of enlightened judgment, not conscience, as a means of determining future activity.

Finally, the enlightened conscience of the strong brother was not actively accusing his deeds, and as a result he was enjoying liberty. Paul recognized that this freedom, due to enlightened conscience, was capable of allowing the man to continue in his deeds until he sinned against the brethren, and consequently, against Christ (1 Cor. 8:10–12).

It becomes clear then that Paul could not advocate any form of dependence upon conscience. Neither the weak conscience (which was overscrupulous), nor the emancipated conscience (which was silent), was of any value at all in the prevention of sin or the choosing of positive activity.

Notes:

1. C. M. Kerr, "Gallio," *International Standard Bible Encyclopaedia*, ed. by James Orr, II (1929), 1167.
2. Ibid.
3. Pierce, *Conscience*, 76.
4. C. S. Beckwith, "Conscience," *The New Schaff-Herzog Encyclopedia of Religious Knowledge*, ed. Samuel Macauley Jackson, III (1952), 242.
5. W. M. Ramsay, "Historical Commentary on the Epistles to the Corinthians," *The Expositor*, 6th series, ed. by W. Robertson Nicoll, I (1900), 97.

6. Ibid., v.

7. Pierce, *Conscience*, 77.

8. Ibid., 76.

9. Archibald Robertson and Alfred Plummer, *A Critical and Exegetical Commentary on the First Epistle of St. Paul to the Corinthians*. 2nd ed. *The International Critical Commentary* (Edinburgh: T. & T. Clark, 1914), 171-72.

10. Bascom, "Syneidesis," 19.

Five

The Alternative to Conscience

Paul's *A Priori* Approach

It has been shown that conscience could not be relied upon as a preventive for sin. Conscience functions as an accuser of guilt after the act has been committed. To rely upon the accusing voice of conscience was the folly of the Corinthians because they used it wrongly. Their's was a negative use of silence as a positive guide, and this depended upon a prior involvement in sin. What was needed was a trustworthy ethic to be used *before* the involvement in improper action. It was ever Paul's concern to avoid sin, not merely to accuse or excuse it after it happened. To this end Paul wrote the Corinthian Epistles. To be sure, he wrote to correct some disorders which were already present (1 Cor. 1:10–17; 5:1–13; 6:1–11; 8:1–13; 11:17–34), but this was to the intent that he might accomplish a positive and progressive work by showing them "a more excellent way" (1 Cor. 12:31). Paul said, "For I am jealous over you with godly jealousy: for I have espoused you to one husband, that I may present you as a chaste virgin to Christ" (2 Cor. 11:2). Note the following statement from 2 Corinthians 13:7–9:

> Now I pray to God that ye do no evil; not that we should appear approved, but that ye should do that which is honest, though we be as reprobates. For we can do nothing against the truth, but for the truth. For we are glad, when we are weak, and ye are strong: and this also we wish, even your perfection.

Thus it is seen that Paul had more in mind than merely helping them solve their problems. He wished to show them a more excellent way, which could provide positive leadership that they may be edified thereby (cf. 2 Cor. 12:19). It is important that attention be placed on living for Christ with affirmations of hope and purpose rather than on restrictions that accompany careful living.

In our modern world there is a great need for positive ideas in concert with Christian carefulness. The larger and more liberal religious groups specialize in the contagious message of universal love and social concern, and they present a positive, attractive image. They do, however, experience difficulty in that they offer little life-changing vitality in spiritual things. Their message of love and self help appeals to the unregenerate population and stimulates interest, but there is still the need for confrontation concerning regeneration. Ecumenical efforts, which are designed to appeal to all people, usually are too general and too nonspecific in doctrinal detail. What is needed is the careful and positive presentation of the complete spectrum of Christian teaching. Such teaching should include distinctions about the plan of salvation and about personal and ecclesiastical separation. The position of the careful Christian should be quite positive in keeping with all that has been provided for him in Christ. The avoidance of sin should be presented and demonstrated as a joyous opportunity to offer loving service to a loving Savior. We love Him because He first loved us and washed us from our sins in His own blood.

In ancient Corinth Paul's major a priori argument was based upon what Christ had done for them. It was the ground of all his appeal, the reason for his expectation and the basis for all his hope for them. He referred to Christ's work many times (1 Cor. 1:2, 4, 9, 10, 13; 2:2, 16; 4:15; 6:11, 14, 20; 8:11; 10:16; 11:23–29; 15:3, 4, 20, 57—just to note a few in the first epistle), and found it to be a strong motivating force. Perhaps the clearest example of this usage is found in 2 Corinthians 5:15–21 and 6:1, 2. On the basis of what he had said in chapter five about being new creatures in Christ, and all things being new and of God, Paul beseeched them to "receive not the grace of God in vain" (2 Cor. 6:1). The word "beseech" is a very interesting word, translating the Greek word *parakaleo,* which means a number of things. It means to "call to one's side, . . . to appeal to, . . . urge, . . . exhort, . . . request, . . . implore, . . . intreat."[1] The word is common in the New Testament and may be taken to mean "to make earnest appeal" or to "beg." It was used in 1 Corinthians 1:10 in Paul's appeal for unity where he appealed to them in the "name of our Lord Jesus Christ." Thus Paul connected his earnest appeal with the work of Christ for them.

The subject of motivation in Christian living should be very much a subject of study and investigation. Thankfulness and appreciation for grace received can and does motivate believers to grateful service in Jesus' name. Realization of God's love for us will win our hearts and our willing and sincere devotion to Him. To realize the awful condition and the condemnation from which we have been delivered will cement our devotion and make disciples of us. In addition, the contemplation of the needs and the condition of those we love and with whom we come into contact often, will urge us to become effective witnesses and careful examples. We have many reasons to love and serve the Lord. It is therefore quite reasonable that Paul should combine an appeal to what Christ had done with an appeal for a positive approach to Christian living.

Throughout the Corinthian epistles, in spite of the scathing response to the evils that were present, the apostle managed to maintain a positive attitude and to present positive arguments. Based upon Christ's love for them, and their love for Christ, Paul made the following statements: "I thank my God always on your behalf . . ." (1 Cor. 1:4); "in everything ye are enriched by Him . . ." (1 Cor. 1:5); "the testimony of Christ was confirmed in you . . ." (1 Cor. 1:6); "of him are ye in Christ Jesus . . ." (1 Cor. 1:30); "we have the mind of Christ . . ." (1 Cor. 2:16); "ye are the temple of God . . . the Spirit of God dwelleth in you . . ." (1 Cor.3:16); "ye are Christ's and Christ is God's" (1 Cor. 3:23); "even Christ our passover is sacrificed for us: Therefore . . ." (1 Cor. 5:7, 8); "But he that is joined unto the Lord is one spirit" (1 Cor. 6:17); "For ye are bought with a price: therefore glorify God in your body, and in your spirit, which are God's" (1 Cor. 6:20). The statements above are but a few, taken from the first six chapters of the first epistle to the Corinthians. However, they clearly demonstrate Paul's positive approach, based upon their relation to Christ and established in love.

Paul turned their use of conscience, which was basically an appeal to a silent conscience after sin was committed, into a forward application of love for the Lord as a basic motive for careful living. Paul also appealed to the love of one Christian for another Christian as a valid motive for modifying behavior. One of the most beautiful chapters in all the Bible is found in the midst of a letter sent to one of the most corrupt churches! Paul showed them what the practical outworking of love for the brethren should be as they conditioned their actions in love. First Corinthians 12 sets forth love as a prime consideration in relating to others when it says: "and yet shew I unto you a more excellent way" (v. 31). Chapter 13 explains: "Love suffereth long, and is kind . . . vaunteth not itself . . . seeketh not her own . . . beareth all things . . . endureth all things . . . never faileth . . ." (1 Cor. 13:4–8). Thus did Paul exhort his readers to "Follow after charity . . ." (1 Cor. 14:1), with a view toward the other person's welfare. Love was Paul's antidote to selfishness, factions, dissention over gifts, immorality, and food offered to idols. Paul's positive emphasis is clearly seen here and throughout the Corinthian epistles as he uses himself as an example of self-giving for the sake of others (1 Cor. 9) and exhorts them to "Be ye followers of me, even as I also am of Christ. Now I praise you, brethren, that ye remember me in all things . . ." (1 Cor. 11:1, 2). Consideration of any proposed act and its anticipated consequences must be conditioned by love and selfless concern for God and for others. **At this point the Christian ethic exerts its authority—the authority of love to constrain and to condition the attitudes and behavior patterns of the believer.**

The Corinthian believers who claimed to have knowledge were certainly in a position to know how the weak brother would feel when assailed by conscience. They had lived by the same views, the same use of conscience, the same Corinthian ethic. Paul appealed to this understanding and directed their attention to the weak brother. He exhorted them to behold what the inconsiderate use of their own freedom from conscience would do to the conscience of him that was weak. This appreciation of the other man's need, conditioned by love as a positive ethic, was expected to evoke a willingness in the mature Corinthian to limit his use of liberty for the benefit of the other man (cf. 1 Cor. 8).

Paul's Emphasis Upon Enlightened Judgment

Throughout this treatment we have emphasized that conscience is not to be regarded as a guide to future behavior. We have seen that conscience is always active after the act, and not before; and that it is always negative or silent, but never positive. What are we to use as we anticipate future activity? The apostle offered the advice that the Corinthians should learn to think ahead about their actions and about the consequences of their deeds. They should learn to make choices based upon their use of judgment rather than upon a vain appeal to silent conscience. The constant use of the phrase "know ye not?" in 1 Corinthians 3:16; 6:2, 3, 9, 15, 16, 19; 9:13, 24; and Paul's appeal to their ability to judge (1 Cor. 2:15, 16; 6:2, 4; 10:15; 11:13, 28, 31) is ample evidence of what they should have done. Paul said: "Know ye not that we shall judge angels? how much more things that pertain to this life?" (1 Cor. 6:3). **Enlightened judgment** was the means by which they were to plan their actions and the means by which we are to plan ours. They were to avoid resorting to the witness of conscience and were told to judge their own actions ahead of time to avoid evil consequences.

It is true that Paul was not satisfied with the state of their enlightened judgment as evidenced by his reference to their carnality in 1 Corinthians 3:1. However, all through chapter two and into chapter three Paul appeals to the teaching of the Holy Spirit (2:13–16) and characterizes the spiritual man as one who judges all things. The apostle provided in the Corinthian Epistles page after page of instruction (over thirty chapters!) to these people for the purpose of further enlightenment, so that they could judge their actions properly in relation to the standards of God.

While we are not to depend upon conscience but upon judgment, we must realize that judgment needs reliable data in order to be of value. We dare not trust intuition or some other feeling for our direction. God has provided a comprehensive statement of His standards in the Bible and the burden is clearly upon the individual believer to study what God has provided. Second Timothy 2:15 says: "Study to shew thyself approved unto God, a workman that needeth not to be ashamed, rightly dividing the word of truth." The Psalmist asks, "Wherewithal shall a young man cleanse his way? by taking heed thereto according to thy word" (Ps. 119:9). Again, "Thy word have I hid in mine heart, that I might not sin against thee" (Ps. 119:11). Again the Psalmist declares, "Teach me good judgment and knowledge: for I have believed thy commandments" (Ps. 119:66). Verses 104 and 105 of this same psalm also help us, "Through thy precepts I get understanding: therefore I hate every false way. Thy word is a lamp unto my feet, and a light unto my path."

The inerrant Word of an omniscient God Who desires our highest good is available to us and we have the opportunity to condition our judgment by studying it and applying its teachings to our lives. We will all stand before the One Who provided the standard for us, and we will give account for what we have done. The Word of God is forever settled in Heaven and every creature will be evaluated by its teachings. We would do well to evaluate all things by what we find in that Book.

There are many well-meaning Christians who feel that they should look elsewhere for approval of their expectations and actions. Some look to denominational headquarters or to respected leaders, hoping to discover what to do or how to feel about things. Some look to friends or family, feeling that their opinions are valid as instruction. Sadly, some look to their own experiences or feelings as justification, just as the Corinthians did, only to find that there is no trustworthy source of information there. Romans 14:5 says: ". . . Let every man be fully persuaded in his own mind," asserting that each of us has the God-given responsibility to use our judgment properly before we act. We are to have confidence in the fact that that which we allow God also allows. Note Romans 14:22: ". . . Happy is he that condemneth not himself in that thing which he alloweth."

At this point the confusion that exists between the so-called antecedent conscience and enlightened judgment should be considered. It has been shown that conscience acts as a judge after a deed has been committed and there is little dispute over this aspect of the work of conscience. The difficulty that some people encounter arises when the function of conscience is confused with the anxiety felt before an act is committed. Some claim that antecedent anxiety is due to the function of conscience when it is actually due to the feedback of judgment. David Seabury has defined this kind of idea as a *coenotrope.* Seabury says: "The delusion that one's conscience, as the word is commonly understood, will reveal what is right and wrong is a coenotrope. . . ."[2] Again he states: "A group of coenotropes working together often create a series of abnormal fear centers that act as a 'voice' as long as the deluded person believes it to be a guide."[3] Thus Seabury traces the so-called antecedent conscience to fear centers. This fear, or anxiety, is the result of considering the logical consequences of an anticipated act, which consideration is the exercise of judgment and is not to be confused with conscience. D. B. Klein, in *Mental Hygiene,* says: "What this means is that the wish is not merely father to the thought of its own gratification, but also to the thought of the results of such gratification."[4] In simple terms, this means that **a person, if normal, will think of the consequences of a proposed act at the same time he anticipates the act.** When one acts without giving thought to the consequences he is sociopathic; that is, he consciously ignores or cares not at all about the results. The normal individual will think about the consequences of a wrong act, which may involve embarrassment, inconvenience, or pain at the same time the act is planned. To consider possible adverse results will bring on the feeling known as anxiety. The fear of getting caught and being punished will prevent a person from performing a wrongful act.

Klein comments on Freud's view: "According to the Freudian formula, anxiety, represented in consciousness by thoughts of dire consequences, brings about repression of the illicit wish."[5] Human reason and judgment are clearly involved, as seen in the following analysis by Klein:

> In schematic terms the sequence of events may be compressed into the following formula: (1) illicit desire; (2) anticipation of both pleasant and unpleasant consequences of gratification; (3) anxiety because of possible threat to emotional security; (4) restraint or repression of desire. This new formula, it will be noted makes anxiety a cause of repression.[6]

Fear, then, acts as a form of motivation that helps to determine avoidance. It is this antecedent anxiety, or fear, that has been confused with conscience. Many well-meaning persons have imagined a "voice," supposedly from conscience, as they anticipated an act. The opposite of the anxiety over a future wrongdoing is the feeling of satisfaction or peace when a decision is made to do the proper act. The feedback of positive judgment concerning the good outcomes of proper acts produces anticipation of satisfaction, which satisfaction is thought to be a "voice" saying "go ahead."

After having said all this about the conscience being unable to lead at any time, there is another aspect of judgment, however, in which the conscience is involved. Acting ahead of time by means of judgment and anticipation, a person can make good use of painful memories to help him choose his acts. When the pain of a guilty conscience has been felt on a previous occasion after a bad act, the memory of the pain can be a strong deterrent. In this sense the conscience, through memory, contributes to judgment concerning acts not yet committed. The individual can remember the pain of conscience that resulted from a past act and can alter his plans to avoid a repetition of the pain that he knows will result from his contemplated deed.

In either case, the anxiety resulting from fear or the memory of the unpleasant past, the judgment of the individual, not his conscience, is the direct agent in the direction of his behavior. Thus it can be seen that the apostle Paul was correctly appealing to the judgment of the Corinthian people, based upon their understanding of what Christ had done for them and upon the consequences of what their actions might do to the conscience of the weak believer.

Paul's Use of Conscience

We have seen the basic approach used by the apostle with the Corinthians and have noted his emphatic appeal to a positive stance, based upon what the Lord had done for them. We have seen his appeal to love as a motive for acceptable behavior—Christ's love for them, their love for Christ, and their love for each other. They were to carefully evaluate the supposed effects of planned actions in appreciation of Christ's work and in appreciation of the bond of love that existed between them.

It is clear in 1 Corinthians 8 that Paul was using the matter of the other person's conscience as a lever to modify the behavior of the one eating meat in the idol's temple. In this use Paul was recognizing the prevalent negative use of conscience and capitalizing on it as an apologetic for the Christian ethic. He was appealing to the pain of conscience as a wound (1 Cor. 8:12), and presenting it as something to be avoided.

There is another use of conscience that should be studied. As we saw in chapter two, Paul was able to say "For I know nothing by myself; yet am I not hereby justified: but he that judgeth me is the Lord" (1 Cor. 4:4). By simply not knowing of guilt, some were assuming that everything they did was acceptable to God. Paul said that he had no knowledge of guilt, but that he was not to assume by that lack of guilt that he had done things of which God approved. He said that he was not justified by his absence of guilt feelings. His justification must come from the Lord and only the Lord's statement could be trusted for justification. In a context that dealt with judging works, Paul said that having a clear conscience did not provide a positive statement that his deeds were good. The tendency of the Corinthians was to interpret a silent conscience to mean that an act was inherently good, and that as a result the person received the approbation of God. The issue centers around the question of the witness of conscience in a context where it is not accusing one of guilt. It has been said above that the conscience either accuses, causing awareness of guilt, or says nothing. How then does it witness to innocence?

In 2 Corinthians Paul undertakes to defend himself against the charges made by some against his character. In this second letter, however, all three uses of the word for conscience are used to assure other people of one's personal integrity. When conscience is called upon to bear an approving testimony, rather than a condemning one, the concept becomes abnormal to the generally understood pagan use. Second Corinthians 1:12 finds the reference to conscience being used in a dependent clause which, in effect, modifies the main clause. Their rejoicing was due to the fact that they had lived in sincerity and simplicity, and that conscience did not accuse them of wrong. In 2 Corinthians 4:2 Paul mentioned their behavior again, and stated that by manifesting the truth they have been commending themselves to every man's conscience. Alford translates this phrase thusly: "with reference to the verdict of every conscience of men. . . ."[7] This is another case of the absence of an accusing conscience. The third and last occurrence also deals with their behavior (2 Cor. 5:11). In effect Paul says here that he and his companions are known to God and to the Corinthians. He is attesting pure motives by declaring that no valid complaint or charge has been made by God, and that none can be made by them. This is another case of their not being able to pronounce a verdict of guilty in their own consciences with reference to Paul.

It is highly significant that in all three of these passages Paul refers to his behavior. It is his behavior that he is attempting to defend in 2 Corinthians, and he does so by pointing out that they cannot accuse him rightly, for to accuse him would bring to themselves the pain of conscience. In none of the verses does Paul say that his conscience approves him. He only says that his conscience agrees with him (says nothing against him) in 2 Corinthians 1:12, and that they can say nothing against him either (2 Cor. 4:2; 5:11). Note that this is again an appeal to a silent conscience. This clearly fits Paul's usage in 1 Corinthians 4:4 where he says his conscience is clear. To assume that the witness of conscience to innocence in 2 Corinthians justifies Paul would be a direct contradiction to his clear statement of 1 Corinthians 4:4 that he was not justified by means of conscience. Thus it can be seen that conscience witnesses to innocence by remaining silent and failing to accuse. To positively state this truth would be to say that he had a good conscience, and that it witnessed to him. A clear example of this dependence upon a silent conscience is found in 1 John 3:21. Here the apostle John uses the word "heart" to refer to conscience (as is often found elsewhere), and makes his evaluation on the basis that there is no condemnation. It is the silent conscience, and not the hypothetical positive or antecedent conscience, that affords confidence toward God.

Paul uses conscience three ways, as seen above. He uses it **to limit the behavior of others, to demonstrate that God is the One to Whom he must look for approval,** and **to answer charges against his character.** All three of these uses relate directly to the needs of the Corinthian people. They had a definite need for the teaching that one should willingly limit his own exercise of liberty for the sake of someone else, and to this end Paul used himself as an example. To Paul, it was important that they learn to look to God for approval, not to conscience.

Paul's third use of conscience relates to his testimony before them, and to their confidence in him and in his message. It was very important to Paul that his testimony among them be not hindered. To this end he made reference to his authority as an apostle (1 Cor. 1:1; 4:9, 21; 7:10; 9:1–12; 11:1, 2; 14:37; 15:1–11; 2 Cor. 1:1; 2:10; 5:20; 10:1–18; 12:11, 12; 13:10). Paul made appeal also to his manner of life among them and was able to say that his conscience was clear (1 Cor. 1: 14–17; 2:1–5; 3:9–11; 4:1–6, 9–13; 8:13; 9:15–27; 10:33; 15:10, 31, 32; 2 Cor. 1:3–10, 12, 23; 2:1–4, 12–17; 4:1—5:13, 16–20; 6:4–10; 7:1–16; 8:19–23; 10:7–18; 11:6–12, 23–31; 12:5–10, 14–19). Paul is saying, in effect, that he has authority and that this authority is authenticated by a proper manner of life. He accented this by referring to something the Corinthians would be sure to understand—the appeal to a clean, clear, good conscience that was void of offense toward God (1 Cor. 4:4; 2 Cor. 1:12; 4:2; 5:11).

Notes:

1. F. Wilbur Gingrich, *Shorter Lexicon of the Greek New Testament* (Chicago: University of Chicago Press, 1957), 161.

2. Seabury, *How Jesus Heals,* 183.

3. Ibid.

4. D. B. Klein, *Mental Hygiene* (New York: Henry Holt and Company, 1944), 536.

5. Ibid., 537.

6. Ibid., 536-37.

7. Henry Alford, *The Greek Testament,* 7th ed. II (Cambridge: Deighton, Bell, and Co., 1874), 650.

SIX

The Cleansing of Conscience

The Need For Cleansing

Many believers are disturbed by the concept that their standing or their security is somehow threatened when they sin. They have the idea that they are secure before God as long as they maintain a good record of obedience or service, but that the record is tarnished or damaged when they sin. Some entertain the concept that there are balance scales of some kind in Heaven, and that their accumulation of guilt renders them vulnerable to exclusion or to some kind of punishment. Believers sometimes carry the burden of thinking that disaster will come, or that illness will come, or that children will be born with defects because God is punishing them for their sins. They feel that they must somehow balance the scales or set the record straight by performing acts of benevolence or charitable deeds of service in the name of the Lord or of the church. When the need for cleansing exists people will lay claim to many supposed means in order to accomplish the task.

Modern society enables us to entertain ourselves, to occupy ourselves, to anesthetize ourselves, to persuade ourselves and to cathart (or empty) ourselves in a vast number of ways. We erroneously suppose that some flurry of religious activity, or some special deed of kindness, or some large contribution to the church will silence our guilty consciences. Nothing could be more incorrect. The Rich Young Ruler of Matthew 19 had done all of these things yet he still had a clear sense of need (Matt. 19:20). The sacrificial system of offerings and sacrifices, used by the Israelites for over a thousand years, could not cleanse the conscience. They offered the blood of bulls and goats faithfully in the Tabernacle:

> Which was a figure for the time then present, in which were offered both gifts and sacrifices, that could not make him that did the service perfect, as pertaining to the conscience (Heb. 9:9).

Those offerings were composed of meats and drinks, and various kinds of washings and ordinances, which were but a shadow of the coming sacrifice of Christ. Note Hebrews 10:1–3:

> For the law having a shadow of good things to come, and not the very image of the things, can never with those sacrifices which they offered year by year continually make the comers thereunto perfect. For then would they not have ceased to be offered? because that the worshippers once purged should have had no more conscience of sins. But in those sacrifices there is a remembrance again made of sins every year.

It is by means of appropriating the value of the shed blood of Christ that the conscience is cleansed. We do not merely wash the outside with ceremonial water as the Hebrews did; instead we claim the precious blood of Christ: "How much more shall the blood of Christ, who through the eternal Spirit offered himself without spot to God, purge your conscience from dead works to serve the living God?" (Heb. 9:14).

But what about the matter of records? What about our service for Christ? What about the gain or loss of rewards? We all know that God keeps records. We are told that several "books" exist in Heaven such as the Lamb's Book of Life (Phil. 4:3; Rev. 3:5; 13:8; 17:8; 21:12, 15; 21:27; 22:19); the seven-sealed book (Rev. 5:1); the little book (Rev. 10:2); and the books out of which the dead are judged (Rev. 21:12). The concept of God as a keeper of records is reinforced by statements concerning the evaluation of works done by believers, such as the Judgment Seat of Christ (Rom. 14:10), where "every one may receive the things done in his body, according to that he hath done, whether it be good or bad" (2 Cor. 5:10). We gain more insight from 1 Corinthians 3:13–15:

> Every man's work shall be made manifest: for the day shall declare it, because it shall be revealed by fire; and the fire shall try every man's work of what sort it is. If any man's work abide which he hath built thereupon, he shall receive a reward. If any man's work shall be burned, he shall suffer loss: but he himself shall be saved; yet so as by fire.

In addition, Jesus spoke of reward in Heaven (Matt. 5:12), and even extended the promise to the giving of a cup of water to a child (Matt. 10:41, 42).

The whole matter of judgment and rewards requires that God know of the activities and motives of every individual. Let us not imagine God as a bespectacled CPA in Heaven bowed over a massive pile of ledgers or as a progressive computer expert who maintains vast memory banks of sophisticated software on each of us. Let us rather understand that we are dealing with the omniscient (all-knowing) God Who already knows all things, whether they be past, present, or future. He does not learn, neither does He forget, in the sense that we learn and forget. All of our deeds and motives are ever present facts before Him, and He has no need for conventional records as we know them. God has used in the Bible the imagery of books and records to teach us that He is aware of all and that all we do will be conscious knowledge to Him when we stand before Him to give an account (cf. Ps. 139).

As believers we are aware that we are living or accumulating a series of behaviors which constitute a record for each of us. There is a clear truth here: namely, that we each compose an accumulated mass of acts and motives, and that we will be confronted with them at some future time. There is some confusion, however, about how our records are to be regarded. The confusion exists because our relation to God has two aspects and we fail to maintain the distinctions between them. The first aspect is *positional*. That is, we are secure as sons who are both born into God's family (John 1:12, 13), and adopted (Gal. 4:4–7). We are actually children of God by faith in Christ Jesus. Our position with God is inviolable because it is based upon and maintained by the work of Jesus Christ for us. He is not only our Savior, but our present Advocate, High Priest, and Intercessor in Heaven with the Father! John 10 says:

> And I give unto them eternal life; and they shall never perish, neither shall any man pluck them out of my hand. My Father, which gave them me, is greater than all; and no man is able to pluck them out of my Father's hand (John 10:28, 29).

The second aspect is *practical* and relates to what kind of children we are. It relates to whether we are obedient or disobedient. It is in this area, the practical and relational, that our sin has its effect rather than in the area of our positional security as sons. Our salvation can never be endangered because our position as sons and daughters in God's family cannot be changed. Our position is based upon a finished transaction in which we were "bought with a price" (1 Cor. 6:20), but our relations and our practical Christian living are not yet finished! It is our fellowship and our communion with the Lord that are affected when we sin against Him. When we become guilty of sin we cannot pray as we should because a matter of disobedience stands between us and God. In every human family the child who disobeys will hang his head and avoid eye contact with the parent. The debtor who defaults or is late meeting his payment responsibilities will avoid the creditor. The conscience points out this matter of unresolved guilt and we feel the pain and experience the sense of resulting spiritual alienation. **In our relationship with the Lord the problem is compounded by the fact that God is too holy to ignore the sin and we are too sinful to confess it.** The need for confession and forgiveness becomes clear as we seek a solution to the problem. Isaiah 59:2, 3 provides an example of how God feels about it:

> But your iniquities have separated between you and your God, and your sins have hid his face from you, that he will not hear. For your hands are defiled with blood, and your fingers with iniquity; your lips have spoken lies, your tongue hath muttered perverseness.

Verse twelve adds: "For our transgressions are multiplied before thee, . . . and as for our iniquities, we know them." The conscious knowledge of guilt will not go away. The memory of violating God's standards will continually bring about the pain of a guilty conscience.

Motives are also a major factor in the believer's relations with God. We waste time and effort and we lose the potential of rewards if our motives are wrong when we perform acts of service. A wrong motive or an act performed as some sort of peace offering to God for sin committed does not qualify as acceptable obedience, and is characterized as "wood, hay, stubble" (1 Cor. 3:12). Works performed by believers who harbor unconfessed sin and are out of fellowship do not atone for sin, do not bring about forgiveness, do not restore fellowship or blessing, and do not cleanse the guilty conscience. Throughout Scripture God requires that the heart of the worshipper be right *before* the service is rendered. God refused the sacrifices mentioned in 1 Samuel 15:22 because of disobedience: "Hath the LORD as great delight in burnt offerings and sacrifices, as in obeying the voice of the LORD? Behold, to obey is better than sacrifice, and to hearken than the fat of rams." Isaiah makes the same point:

> Bring no more vain oblations; incense is an abomination unto me; the new moons and sabbaths, the calling of assemblies, I cannot away with; it is iniquity, even the solemn meeting. Your new moons and your appointed feasts my soul hateth: they are a trouble unto me; I am weary to bear them. And when ye spread forth your hands, I will hide mine eyes from you: yea, when ye make many prayers, I will not hear: your hands are full of blood (Isa. 1:13–15).

Clearly, God seeks the right relationship of heart obedience before the service is considered valid. Believers must serve with a clear, clean, silent conscience if their service is to be acceptable to God.

What is Defiled When We Sin?

Many well-meaning but uninstructed Christians feel that their position before God and their security with God are defiled when they sin. They feel that they can lose their salvation and reverse the work of regeneration in them. Thus, they feel that they may become unregenerate persons again. This is clearly impossible when we consider the presence and work of the Holy Spirit. The Holy Spirit places believers into one Body, the Body of Christ (1 Cor. 12:13), and He does so by the washing of regeneration and renewing of the Holy Ghost (Titus 3:5). This renewing initiates indwelling and is true of all regenerated persons (Rom. 8:9). The Holy Spirit, Who effects regeneration and indwells believers, must somehow be taken from the individual and the effects of His work eradicated if one is to become unregenerated again. Not only is this logically impossible, it is Biblically impossible! According to John 14:16, the Comforter, who is the Holy Spirit, abides forever. Therefore, to fear losing the Holy Spirit is not a valid consideration; and to feel that salvation can be endangered by sin is not valid either.

There is a sense, however, in which the Holy Spirit can be affected by sin in the life of a believer. Ephesians 4:30 states: "And grieve not the holy Spirit of God, whereby ye are sealed unto the day of redemption." Apparently the Spirit can be made to feel what is described as grief. With the Spirit indwelling each of us we are constantly forced to relate all activity to His presence; consequently, when we sin we do not do so in isolation. We can easily understand how the sins of a drunken alcoholic father will affect the family living in the same house with him; can we not also see the effects of our sins on the Holy One Who lives in us? The great sense of defilement that occurs when a sensitive believer sins is produced by the conscience reacting to the knowledge that grief has been forced upon One Who loves us with an everlasting love; One Who feels our pain; One Who knows our every thought; One Whose role is to comfort us in our grief.

It is therefore not our standing with God that is damaged by sin, but our fellowship. Two cannot walk together except they be agreed. It is not the record but the sinner who is defiled. Our minds are defiled with impure and improper thoughts and our hearts are defiled with covetous desires and lust. Our hands are defiled as we involve ourselves in improper acts. In all of this conscience is aroused and points out guilt as it reacts to what is known of the standards of God. **It is not the record that must be cleansed but the individual who must be cleansed.** It is not the law of God but our violating of that law that brings pain. Somehow the accusing finger of conscience must be put to rest, and that can only be accomplished by the cleansing of the individual who has sinned.

How to Claim God's Cleansing

Having a guilty conscience is not something to be taken lightly or to be ignored. Conscience is one of the most powerful motivational forces known to man. Thousands have committed suicide because they could no longer live with the urgings of a guilty conscience. Thieves have surrendered many years after the commission of a crime because of the gnawing pain of conscience. Conscience will relentlessly stalk the path of the unfaithful marriage partner and fill every waking moment with remorse. Countless individuals have afflicted themselves in various physical and psychological ways because they felt the guilt and knew they should be punished. It is quite true that Christians, also, will reach out to many and varied substitutes in order to be rid of the pain of conscience. The Bible affords many examples of persons who have done something wrong and have carried the guilt and pain. Perhaps just a few would illustrate the point: Joseph's brothers sold him into a life of slavery in Egypt, only to repent later with the painful memory of his cries of anguish in the pit; Peter went out and wept bitterly because he had denied (lied about) the Lord and had cursed and sworn deceitfully; Judas, who betrayed the Lord, first tried to give back the money and undo what he had done, but was unable to do so; so he killed himself. **Conscience is no respecter of persons and it can only be silenced by delusion, diversion or cleansing.** The first two, delusion and diverison, are incomplete and temporary and offer no real solution to the problem.

The key New Testament passage on the subject of cleansing is 1 John 1:9, which says: "If we confess our sins, he is faithful and just to forgive us our sins, and to cleanse us from all unrighteousness." Two important points are to be made initially as we consider the verse: (1) God has offered cleansing and forgiveness to believers. It is there to be claimed. (2) The means for obtaining cleansing and forgiveness is clearly stated in the verse, namely confession. What does confession mean? What does it imply? Does God expect a long dissertation from every sinning child of His, as though He must somehow be persuaded to forgive? The answer is "no." To confess means to "say the same thing," or to "agree," and in the case of sin, to agree with God about it. If God has pointed out in His Word that what you have done is wrong, and you are aware of your sin, the procedure then is to yield to Him in such a manner as to say "yes," telling God that you recognize Him to be right, that what you have done is sin. To truly confess is to adopt the same attitude toward your sin that God has toward it, to change your mind (repent) about it, and to despise it. To agree with God, then, is the nature of true confession, and it involves a change of attitude toward the sin. If a person sins and then goes through the motions of confession without the change of attitude, full well knowing that he is going to do that same sin again, he has not confessed at all. Complacent confession does not fit the picture of true confession. One cannot adopt a take-it-or-leave-it attitude toward sin and at the same time share God's feelings about sin.

In the verse before us, 1 John 1:9, forgiveness and cleansing are based upon two things: the faithfulness and justice of God. The Bible does not say that God is loving and kind to forgive us our sins. God certainly is a loving, kind, and gracious God, but the basis for forgiveness and cleansing which He would have us understand in the verse is His *faithfulness* and *justice*. That means that God, due to His faithfulness, cannot deny Himself. He must keep His word and do what He says He will do. He is also just; therefore He must always do the right things. The right thing for God to do is to recognize the work of Jesus Christ on behalf of believers; observe: The Bible teaches that Jesus Christ is the propitiation for our sins (Rom. 3:25), and that God has set Him forth as the sufficient payment for all of our sins. It follows that if God has exacted payment for all of our sins from Him, it would be unjust for God to require us to pay for them again. Since God has punished Jesus in our place for all of our sins, He cannot ever punish us for any one of them. We could not pay for a single sin, even if we wanted to. If a believer ever had to pay for a single sin for which Christ died, the whole ship of substitution would be blown right out of the water! God must forgive when the condition of confession has been met because the debt has been paid, and God's own righteous character demands that He forgive.

The fact that God reminds us that forgiveness and cleansing are based on His faithfulness and justice is in itself a gracious blessing. God provides us with the clear assurance that cleansing does not depend on our degree of spirituality, our ability to realize His presence, our record of faithfulness, or on any other thing we might offer as an inducement to Him to forgive us. He forgives *freely*, based upon the provision He has made in Christ when we approach Him with a broken and a contrite heart, realizing the fact of our sin and regarding it as God regards it. God is not capricious or arbitrary; He is consistent and unchanging. His Word can be believed and trusted at all times.

There is a sense in which God will allow adversity to come into the lives of sinning believers. Hebrews 12:5–11 speaks of the chastening activity of God in the lives of those He loves:

> And ye have forgotten the exhortation which speaketh unto you as unto children, My son, despise not thou the chastening of the Lord, nor faint when thou art rebuked of him: for whom the Lord loveth he chasteneth, and scourgeth every son whom he receiveth (vv. 5, 6).

Also, verse eleven says: "Now no chastening for the present seemeth to be joyous, but grievous: nevertheless afterward it yieldeth the peaceable fruit of righteousness unto them which are exercised thereby." **God does chasten believers, and it is always with a view to their development and edification, never punishment.** Some are weak and sickly, and many sleep in death (1 Cor. 11:30) as a result of the chastening hand of God. Obviously, in the case of death (as here and in Acts 5) God removes believers to Heaven, denying them the opportunity for service and using them as object lessons to others. We need to keep "short accounts," that is to confess early and often that we might be blessed and claim opportunities for service and fellowship. The alternative is to require our loving Father to chasten us ". . . for our profit, that we might be partakers of his holiness" (Heb. 12:10).

Accepting Cleansing

Accepting cleansing as fact is a very practical matter. **Many are unable to gain victory when they have confessed and been forgiven simply because they are unable to believe that cleansing has taken place.** Have you ever prayed for cleansing and forgiveness and gone your way only to have the problem of lingering guilt and doubt? You are not alone. If the transgression has been a serious one in terms of social consequences the impression of guilt is much greater. For example, the murderer will recognize and feel guilt much more than the gentle old lady who tells "white lies." If guilt has been burned into your consciousness by difficult circumstances and it is common knowledge to many, it would seem much too simple a solution to simply confess the matter to obtain forgiveness and cleansing. Please remember at this point that **true confession is not arbitrary, but inseparably tied to heart-felt repentance.** When true confession takes place God must forgive because He is just, and also because He is faithful. He must do what He has said He will do. In remaining consistent with His own perfections, God has bound Himself by His promises.

Lingering guilt, or a conscience that will not be silent even after confession and cleansing, is basically the result of unbelief. We simply have difficulty believing that the matter has been resolved. We believe the Word of God when it speaks of things such as Heaven, hell, the deity of Christ, the Virgin Birth, the death, burial, and resurrection of the Lord, and many other things that seem hard to understand and difficult to believe, yet we have trouble when it comes to forgiveness. The reason lies in the fact that forgiveness is freely given. Mankind is habituated to the idea of restitution and that one must pay for or pay back to resolve debt and to clear a matter. We mistakenly think that our sin or misdeed is not being "paid back" when we merely confess. It is like going to the bank and saying "I'm sorry that I did not make my payment," and hearing the banker say "That's all right, you don't have to pay it." To solve the problem we must believe that Jesus has already paid for *all* of our sins. We somehow find it easier to believe that He has paid for our past sins than to believe that He has paid for our future sins and present sins. We have but to believe that Christ has paid for all and that God is quite free to forgive us, based upon Christ's suffering and not ours. We must realize that all of our sins were yet future at the time of Christ's suffering, and that He was consciously accepting the penalty for every one of them.

We do have peace and we are relieved from the lingering pain of a disturbed conscience when we confess and actually believe that God has been faithful to Himself and forgiven us. If you want peace you must believe what God has said about the matter and that He has done what He said. And finally, it must be pointed out that the actual cleansing, as far as God is concerned, takes place whether we believe it or not. That is, God is satisfied when we confess because He rightly appreciates the value of Christ's death even when we do not. The lingering guilt we feel is because of *our* limitations, not His. Conscience will rest when knowledge of forgiveness becomes sure. Just as surely as ". . . perfect love casteth out fear" (1 John 4:18), proper confidence in God's work of cleansing will cast out the pain of a guilty conscience. Let us not look for feelings of some kind as proof of forgiveness, let us rather believe what the Eternal One has said about it. The cure for a guilty conscience, according to 1 John 1:9, is to confess our sins and trust that God has taken care of the matter completely. Then, and only then, can we get up off our knees and hold our heads up with confidence and go on and live for God.

Seven

Conclusion

The Nature of Conscience

This study began with an investigation of the nature of conscience in man. It was found that *suneidesis* referred, as a noun, to a faculty in man and not to a frequentative response of the individual to a violation of moral standards. Every man has a conscience (Rom. 2:15) that is capable of effecting in him a clear sense of his shortcomings. Conscience is seen to be a judge that reacts to violations of social, moral, and religious standards. The use of conscience at Corinth was more restricted than that which is used in modern times. Modern usage considers conscience to be some sort of general obligation with moral connotations, which is capable of directing with reference to future behavior. The Corinthians saw conscience as an accuser of guilt, without reference to a supposed antecedent ability to direct the individual.

It appears that conscience was mostly negative in its role, and operated not as an independent and volitionally operative agent, but as an automatic built-in accuser over which man had no authority. A man was not guilty until he had acted, so a negative, accusing conscience could not operate until he was, in fact, guilty. Conscience, then, always operates subsequent to the act and is negative in content. On the other hand, a good conscience equals no sense of guilt or no accusation of wrong. A clear conscience is one which is void of offense. The good or approving conscience witnesses by means of silence, and it is said to approve when it fails to witness to any guilt. A clean or clear conscience is not to be depended upon as a means of justification for an act (1 Cor. 4:4).

This faculty called conscience can be identified by its response to acts that are contrary to standards that have been learned by the individual. Conscience can be conditioned by stimuli external to the individual, such as the teachings of home, church, school, and society at large. The conscience of the Corinthians was conditioned by culture, by its own pagan philosophy, by its current religious practices, and by social considerations.

The Place of Conscience

To discover the Biblical use of conscience we found it necessary to study its operation at Corinth. The Corinthian people were allowed personal liberties while under the rule of the Romans, and these liberties were governed by a negative appeal to conscience. Their social and religious conscience had been sufficiently conditioned so as to render it useless, except in civil matters. When Paul established the church at Corinth, he provided a body of Christian teaching which served as a standard by which the conscience of the Christian people there could operate. During Paul's absence of about five years (ca. A.D. 50-55), the Corinthian church had learned to depend upon the negative use of their Christianized conscience. This state is represented in the Corinthian Epistles. Many problems had arisen in the church and they had appealed to Paul for help (1 Cor. 7:1). He answered by pointing out their errors and providing extensive doctrinal instruction. One of Paul's main thrusts was to demonstrate to the Corinthians that they were not to depend upon the negative use of conscience. He pointed out that an overscrupulous conscience, characterized as a weak conscience, can torment the weak brother unnecessarily as a result of the misuse of the liberty of the brother who has knowledge. The weak conscience is not to be desired. But what of the emancipated conscience of the one who had knowledge? Paul pointed out (1 Cor. 8) that the conscience that had been liberated by the knowledge that an idol was nothing did not act to remind the brother of his wrong; therefore it could not prevent the misuse of liberty. The emancipated conscience remained silent, and was surely not to be depended upon.

The *Praxis* of Conscience

Paul, recognizing the situation, presented the Christian ethic as an approach which was positive rather than negative. He based his exhortations on the fact of their salvation and on their appreciation of what Christ had done for them. He desired to present them as a "chaste virgin to Christ" (2 Cor. 11:2), and not merely to solve problems. His appeal was along two main lines: First, he appealed to their enlightened judgment as a guide to future action and not to their dependence upon a negative and silent conscience. Judgment acts antecedently but conscience does not, because it either condemns a past act or remains silent. Second, Paul recognized that their judgment needed to be conditioned by love. The authority of the Christian ethic is that of love for Christ and for the Christian brother, and Paul built his case for the limiting of personal liberty on that basis. As seen in 1 Corinthians 13, love is the highest of the Christian virtues and is to be diligently pursued.

Finally, Paul made use of the silent conscience that was well known to the Corinthians as a means of conditioning their behavior, but was careful to point out that they were not to claim justification by it. He also showed that approval was to be sought from God and not from conscience. Paul also appealed to his own manner of life in defense of his apostleship, and backed up his claim to a proper manner of life by stating that his conscience was void of offense.

Conscience, then, is not to be used as a means of direction. God has given us the ability to judge our actions antecedently, or beforehand, and has provided us with the Bible and its teaching and preaching by which we can enlighten and condition our judgment. Our judgment is to be controlled by our love for Christ and for our brethren. Conscience waits silently in the wings—just in case!

We have seen that God has provided a means for the cleansing of a guilty conscience and that gracious provision is based upon the value of the shed blood of Jesus Christ to cleanse us from all sin. We have noted that the condition for cleansing is true confession and not personal feelings of remorse or acts of restitution. We have rejoiced in the fact that forgiveness is tied to the faithfulness and to the justice of God, and we can be confident that He keeps His word and considers us to be sufficiently cleansed when we have confessed. And, finally, we have seen that we must believe what God has said about our cleansing if we are to be free from unnecessary lingering guilt.

Let us resolve that our consciences shall be kept silent by our enlightened obedience to those standards that God has graciously provided for us, and that we will claim every opportunity to exert a positive influence for Christ based upon love. Let us be led by the Word of God and by the Spirit of God, and gladly accept the responsibility to use our enlightened judgment for His glory.

Bibliography

Books

Athenaeus *Deipnosophistae*. Loeb Classical Library, Vol. VI. Translated by C.B. Gulick. London; 1937.

Baird, William. *The Corinthian Church—A Biblical Approach to Urban Culture.* New York: Abingdon Press, 1964.

Barnes, Albert. *Notes, Explanatory and Practical, on The First Epistle of Paul to the Corinthians.* New York: Harper & Brothers, 1854.

_________ . *Scenes and Incidents in the Life of the Apostle Paul.* Grand Rapids: Baker Book House, 1950.

Botsford, George Willis, and Robinson, Charles Alexander, Jr. *Hellenic History.* 3rd ed. New York: The MacMillan Company, 1922.

Burton, Edward. *An Inquiry Into the Heresies of the Apostolic Age.* Oxford: J. Parker and C. and J. Rivington, 1829.

Chafer, Lewis Sperry. *Systematic Theology.* 8 vols. Dallas: Dallas Seminary Press, 1947.

Coneybeare, W. J., and Howson, J. S. *The Life and Epistles of Saint Paul.* New York: George H. Doran Company, n.d.

Delitzsch, Franz. *A System of Biblical Psychology.* 2nd ed. Translated by Robert Ernest Wallis. Edinburgh: T. and T. Clark, 1899.

DePressense, E. *Heresy and Christian Doctrine.* London: Hodder and Stoughton, 1873.

Durant, Will. *The Life of Greece.* New York: Simon and Schuster, Inc., 1939.

Eickman, Walther. *Pilgrim Paul.* West New York, New Jersey: Landeck Press, Inc., 1934.

Enslin, Morton Scott. *The Ethics of Paul.* New York: Abingdon Press, 1957.

Fisher, George P. *The Beginnings of Christianity.* New York: Charles Scribner's Sons, 1905.

Fletcher, Joseph F. *Situation Ethics.* Philadelphia: Westminster Press, 1966.

Glover, Terrot Reaveley. *Greek Byways.* New York: The MacMillan Company, 1932.

Hallesby, O. *Conscience.* Translated by Clarence J. Carlsen. Minneapolis: Augsburg Publishing House, 1933.

Klein. D. B. *Mental Hygiene.* New York: Henry Holt and Company, 1944.

Longenecker, Richard N. *Paul, Apostle of Liberty.* New York: Harper & Row, 1964.

M'Clintock, John, and Strong, James., eds. *Cyclopaedia of Biblical, Theological, and Ecclesiastical Literature.* 10 vols. Harper & Brothers, 1873.

Metzger, Henri. *St. Paul's Journeys in the Greek Orient.* London: SCM Press, Ltd., 1954.

Ogg, George. *The Chronology of the Life of Paul.* London: Epworth Press, 1968.

Pausanius *Description of Greece.* Loeb Classical Library, I. Translated by W. H. S. Jones. London: 1927.

Pierce, C. A. *Conscience in the New Testament.* London: SCM Press, Ltd., 1955.

Ramsay, William Mitchell. *St. Paul the Traveller and the Roman Citizen.* 15th ed. London: Hodder and Stoughton, Limited, 1925.

Robinson, W. Gordon. *The Gospel and the Church in a Pagan World.* London: Independent Press Ltd., 1958.

Seabury, David. *How Jesus Heals Our Minds Today.* Boston: Little, Brown and Company, 1949.

Strabo *Geography.* Loeb Classical Library, IV. Translated by H. L. Jones. London: 1927.

Tixeront, J. *History of Dogmas.* Translated from 5th French ed. Vol. I. St. Louis: B. Herder Book Company, 1930.

Wallbank, T. Walter, and Taylor, Alastair M. *Civilization Past and Present.* Chicago: Scott, Foresman and Company, 1956.

Wilson. R. McL. *Gnosis and the New Testament.* Oxford: Basil Blackwell, 1968.

Texts

Aland, Kurt; Black, Matthew; Metzger, Bruce M.; and Wikgren, Allen, eds. *The Greek New Testament.* New York: American Bible Society, 1966.

Holy Bible. American Standard Version. New York: Thomas Nelson & Sons, 1901.

Kittel, Rudolf, ed. *Biblia Hebraica.* 7th ed. Stuttgart: Wurttembergische Bibelanstalt, 1951.

Scofield, C. I., ed. *The New Scofield Reference Bible: Holy Bible.* New York: Oxford University Press, 1967.

Lexical Aids

Brown, Francis; Driver, S. R.; Briggs, Charles A. *A Hebrew and English Lexicon of the Old Testament.* Oxford: Clarendon Press, 1907.

Feyerabend, Karl. *Langenscheidt's Pocket Hebrew Dictionary.* New York: Barnes & Noble, Inc., 1961.

Hatch, Edwin, and Redpath, Henry A. *A Concordance to the Septuagint.* 2 vols. Oxford: Clarendon Press, 1897.

Lampe, G. W. H., ed. *A Patristic Greek Lexicon.* Oxford: Clarendon Press, 1961.

Liddell, Henry George; Scott, Robert; and Jones, Henry Stuart. *A Greek-English Lexicon.* 9th ed. Oxford: At the Clarendon Press, 1940.

Moulton, W.F., and Geden, A. S. *A Concordance to the Greek Testament.* Edinburgh: T. & T. Clark, 1897.

Sophocles, Evangelinus A. *Greek Lexicon of the Roman and Byzantine Periods.* 2 vols. New York: Frederick Ungar Publishing Company, n.d.

Commentaries

Hodge, Charles. *An Exposition of the First Epistle to the Corinthians.* New York: Robert Carter & Brothers, 1857.

Plummer, Alfred. *A Critical and Exegetical Commentary on the Second Epistle of St. Paul to the Corinthians. The International Critical Commentary.* Edited by S. R. Driver, A. Plummer and C. A. Briggs. Edinburgh: T. & T. Clark, 1915.

Robertson, Archibald T. *Word Pictures in the New Testament.* 6 vols. Nashville: Broadman Press, 1930-33.

________ ., and Plummer, Alfred. *A Critical and Exegetical Commentary on the First Epistle of St. Paul to the Corinthians.* 2nd ed. *The International Critical Commentary.* Edited by S. R. Driver, A. Plummer and C. A. Briggs. Edinburgh: T. & T. Clark, 1914.

Sanday, William, and Headlam, Arthur C. *A Critical and Exegetical Commentary on the Epistle to the Romans.* 5th ed. *The International Critical Commentary.* Edited by S. R. Driver, A. Plummer and C. A. Briggs. Edinburgh: T. and T. Clark, 1902.

Simon, W. G. H. *The First Epistle to the Corinthians.* London: SCM Press Ltd., 1959.

Encyclopaedia and Periodical Articles

Barnhouse, Donald Grey. "Can You Trust Your Conscience?" *Eternity Magazine,* (September, 1961), 20, 21.

Bascom, John. "Conscience, its Relations and Office." *Bibliotheca Sacra,* XXIV (1867), 150-175.

Beckwith, C. A. "Conscience." *The New Schaff-Herzog Encyclopaedia of Religious Knowledge.* Edited by Samuel Macauley Jackson, II (1952), 242-44.

Broneer, Oscar. "Corinth, Center of St. Paul's Missionary Work in Greece," *Biblical Archaeologist,* XIV (December, 1951), 78-96.

"Conscience." *Encyclopaedia Britannica.* (1969). Vol. VI.

Davies, W. D. "Conscience," *The Interpreter's Dictionary of the Bible.* I (1962), 671-76.

Harris, B. F. "Syneidesis in the Pauline Writings," *Westminster Theological Journal,* XXIV (1962), 173-86.

Harry, J. E. "Corinth." *International Standard Bible Encyclopaedia.* Edited by James Orr, II (1929), 710-11.

Kahler, M. "Conscience." *The New Schaff-Herzog Encyclopedia of Religious Knowledge.* Edited by Samuel Macauley Jackson. IV (1952), 242-43.

Kerr, C. M. "Gallio." *International Standard Bible Encyclopaedia.* Edited by James Orr, II (1929), 1167-68.

Kik, J. Marcellus. "The Christian and His Conscience." *Christianity Today,* (April 24, 1964), 28-29.

Knight, James A. "Conscience." *Union Seminary Quarterly Review,* XIX (January, 1964), 131-9.

MacDonald, William A. "Archaeology and St. Paul's Journeys in Greek Lands, Part III: Corinth," *Biblical Archaeologist,* V (September, 1942), 36-48.

Mason, Clarence E. "A Study of Pauline Motives." *Bibliotheca Sacra,* CXI (1954), 213-28.

Nauss, Allen. "Freud's Superego and the Biblical Syneidesis." *Concordia Theological Monthly,* XXXIII (May, 1962), 273-82.

Newell, William R. "Guilt." *Bibliotheca Sacra,* IX (1953), 242-47.

Pelkonen, J. Peter. "The Teachings of John Calvin on the Nature and Function of Conscience." *The Lutheran Quarterly,* XXI (February, 1969), 74-88.

Press, S. D. "Stephanas." *International Standard Bible Encyclopaedia.* Edited by James Orr, V (1929), 2850.

Ramsay, W. M. "Historical Commentary on the Epistles to the Corinthians." *The Expositor,* 6th series, ed. by W. Robertson Nicoll, I (1900), 91-111.

Rees, T. "Epicureans." *International Standard Bible Encyclopaedia.* Edited by James Orr, II (1929), 2854-55.

Rehwinkel, Alfred M. "Conscience." *Baker's Dictionary of Theology.* Edited by Everett F. Harrison (1960), 136-37.

Seitz, Oscar J. F. "Two Spirits in Man: An Essay in Biblical Exegesis." *New Testament Studies,* VI (1959-60), 82-95.

Stalker, James. "Conscience." *International Standard Bible Encyclopaedia.* Edited by James Orr, II (1929), 701-3.
Thrall, Margaret E. "The Pauline Use of *Suneidesis.*" *New Testament Studies,* XIV (1967), 118-25.
Witmer, John A. "Christian Social Responsibility." *Bibliotheca Sacra,* CX (1953), 206-19.
Zuck, Roy B. "The Doctrine of the Conscience." *Bibliotheca Sacra* CXXVI (October-December, 1969), 329-40.

Unpublished Materials

Ashcraft, Roy Neil. "The Historical Setting of I Corinthians." Unpublished Th.M. thesis, Dallas Theological Seminary, 1958, 71.
Bascom, John Carroll. "Syneidesis in the New Testament." Unpublished Th. M. thesis, Dallas Theological Seminary, 1962, 112.
Congdon, Roger D. "The Doctrine of Conscience." Unpublished Th. M. thesis, Dallas Theological Seminary, 1945, 83.
Hawkins, Tom R. "Christian Liberty in the Corinthian Epistles." Unpublished Th. M. thesis, Dallas Theological Seminary, 1969, 72.
Johnson, Samuel Lewis, Jr. "A Survey of Biblical Psychology in the Epistle to the Romans." Unpublished Th.D. dissertation, Dallas Theological Seminary, 1947, ix+223.
Taylor. Elmer H. "The Doctrine of Carnality in First Corinthians." Unpublished Th.M. thesis, Dallas Theological Seminary, 1958, 64.